Life le
Wisd
Motivation

Each person starts out as a caterpillar and through wisdom and experience develops into a butterfly.
- M.I. Seka – 1972 - ; Author & businessman.

Insightful, Enlightened and Inspirational quotations and proverbs.

Compiled by M.I Seka
2015

Volume I, *II*, *III*, *IV*

Providential Press
Phoenix, Arizona

Copyright © 2014 by M.I. Seka
Published by arrangement Providential Press

Inquiries should be addressed to
misekabooks@gmail.com
Facebook: M.I. Seka
Twitter: @misekabooks
Linkedin: M.I. Seka

Cover Design: Paul Alex Condie
www.wix.com/paulalexc/portfolio

ISBN-13:978-1495395635
ISBN-10:1495395634

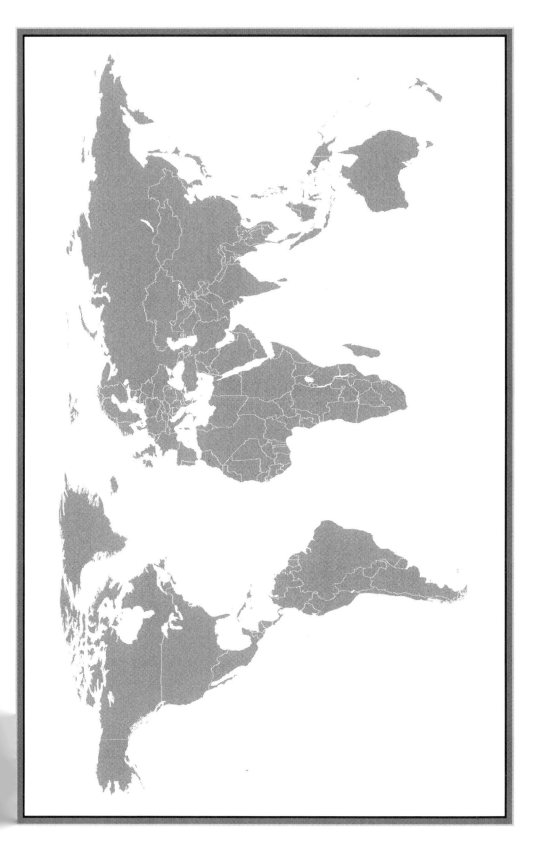

Proverb – a short popular saying, usually of unknown and ancient origin. Thoughtfully expressing a common and universal truth.

Careful consideration has been taken to only use photo's in the public domain whose, copyright has expired.

Read Me First:

While other quote or proverb books give you a scattershot of information based on wording for the purpose of reference or are written purely for entertainment, the quotes and proverbs in these volumes have been carefully chosen to enlighten, elicit thought, expose the most meaningful elements of life, and to inspire you into action. Gathered to give you, the reader, that "Ah ha" feeling that provides that moment of deep thought, clarity, and reflection to help stimulate your mind to new possibilities while clearing up visions of your ideal life.

Taken from the wisest people that ever walked our small planet throughout the ages, these quotes and proverbs are timeless nuggets of wisdom passed down since people were able to comprehend life and the world around them. Although some of the quotes were said over 3,000 years ago, they still hold true even in today's modern times. Surprisingly, some of the same wisdom that held true in ancient times has been repeated throughout history, said in a particular way based on the era, which gives them a heavy weight of truth.

The aim of this huge collection of human wisdom in a word is enlightenment. To assist the readers in realizing what is truly important in their life as well as to find their true self. To shatter the illusions of life that everyone builds for themselves by their false assumptions and stereotypes. To find their true inner being, find purpose, and most importantly, to discover what makes them and them alone happy.

It would be a mistake to concentrate on only one topic or subject because all the headings are connected to aid you in reaching your own insight and enlightenment. Many of the most profound quotes and proverbs are recorded under various topics throughout the book. While you may only be interested in "Success & Failure," many of the quotes and proverbs that are attributed to success can also be found under "Leadership," "Attitude," or even "Life, Purpose, & Growth," for example.

To get the full benefit of these volumes and to fully immerse yourself in <u>self-discovery,</u> you must commit yourself to studying all the sections as well as all the volumes. If you want to scratch the surface of what is important in life, then read 1 volume-but if you want to master what's important in life and your being then study all 4 volumes.

While no one on Earth is special, everyone is unique. Nobody past, present, or future has gone through or has had the same thoughts and experiences as you, nor will they in the future. As a result, you see the world in a completely unique way. Studying these volumes will guide your mind's eye in distinguishing the most significant passages to you and your being as well as reaffirming or contradicting what you already know and believe, by the wisest people throughout history. Out of the thousands of quotes and proverbs in these volumes, your personality and insight will subconsciously pick out the most relevant quotes and proverbs to you and you alone.

I've had similar experience in researching and compiling these volumes. One of the quotes that stuck out for me was "**The only sin is mediocrity.**" (- *Martha Graham 1894 – 1991; American modern dancer, choreographer & Presidential Medal of Freedom recipient.*)

 I've always believed this subconsciously. Reading it clarified and reaffirmed my feelings.

To truly gain from these slices of wisdom, you must commit yourself to study and reflection. Doing so will benefit you tremendously in helping you clarify what is truly important in your life.

We spend so much time and energy on things that won't matter in 1 year, 5 years, or even 10 years, but the wisdom in these pages will last you a lifetime. Taking one month out of your life to figure things out is a very small price to pay for a lifetime of wisdom, enlightenment, and direction.

I've provided several empty pages for you to take notes on the most relevant quotes and proverbs to you. Quotes and proverbs specifically chosen to wake you up, plan, & motivate action into improving your life and happiness.

Each player must accept the cards life deals him or her: but once they are in hand, he or she alone must decide how to play the cards in order to win the game.

- Voltaire (Francois-Marie Arouet) 1694 – 1778; French writer, historian, philosopher, & poet.

~Notes~

~Notes~

~Notes~

~Notes~

~Age~

Age is an issue of mind over matter. If you don't mind, it doesn't matter.
- Mark Twain (Samuel Langhorne Clemens) 1835-1910; American author & humorist.

I must confess I was born at a very early age.
- Groucho Marx (Julius Henry Marx) 1890 – 1977; American comedian and film & TV star.

Age and poverty are ill to bear.
– Lombard Proverb

Virtue is relative to the actions and ages of each of us in all that we do.
- Plato 428 BC – 347 BC; Greek philosopher, mathematician, founder of Academy of Athens (the first institute of higher learning), student of Socrates & teacher of Aristotle.

As we grow old, the beauty steals inward.
- Ralph Waldo Emerson 1803-1882; American lecturer, poet, & essayist.

Old men are dangerous: it doesn't matter to them what is going to happen to the world.
- George Bernard Shaw 1856 – 1950; Irish playwright, co-founder of London School of Economics, critic, journalist, Nobel Prize winner, & Oscar winner.

Middle age is when you've met so many people that every new person you meet reminds you of someone else.
- Frederic Ogden Nash 1902 – 1971; American poet.

How old would you be if you didn't know how old you was?
- Satchel Paige 1906 – 1982; American hall of fame baseball player.

Old age, believe me, is a good and pleasant thing. It is true you are gently shouldered off the stage, but then you are given such a comfortable front stall as spectator.

- Confucius 551 BC – 479 BC; Chinese teacher, politician, & philosopher.

If youth knew; if age could.

- Sigmund Freud 1856 – 1939; Austrian Neurologist, & founder of Psychoanalysis.

Nobody grows old merely by living a number of years. We grow old by deserting our ideals. Years may wrinkle the skin, but to give up enthusiasm wrinkles the soul.

- Samuel Ullman 1840 – 1924; American businessman, poet, & humanitarian.

The more sand has escaped from the hourglass of our life, the clearer we should see through it.

- Niccolo Machiavelli 1469 – 1527; Italian historian, politician, diplomat, philosopher, & writer.

There is a fountain of youth: it is your mind, your talents, the creativity you bring to your life and the lives of people you love. When you learn to tap this source, you will truly have defeated age.

- Sophia Loren (Sofia Villani Scicolone) 1934 - ; Italian actress.

Intelligent life on a planet comes of age when it first works out the reason for its own existence.

- Richard Dawkins 1941 - ; English author, ethologist, & evolutionary biologist.

The trick is growing up without growing old.

- Casey Stengel 1890 – 1975; American major league baseball player, hall of fame inductee.

Middle age is youth without levity, and age without decay.
- Doris Day (Doris Mary Ann Kappelhoff) 1924 - ; American film & TV actress, singer, animal rights activist.

I can feel the 60S looming. In my profession, I've just moved along with my age. By thinking in decades, rather than whether someone's 42 or 47, you can give yourself a whole 10 years to turn yourself around in.
- Francesca Annis 1945 – English actress.

While one finds company in himself and his pursuits, he cannot feel old, no matter what his years may be.
- Amos Bronson Alcott 1799 – 1888; American teacher, writer, philosopher, abolitionist, and reformer.

Men of age object too much, consult too long, adventure too little, repent too soon, and seldom drive business home to the full period, but content themselves with a mediocrity of success.
- Dale Carnegie 1888 – 1955; American writer, lecturer, & self-improvement coach.

Not to expose your true feelings to an adult seems to be instinctive from the age of seven or eight onwards.
- George Orwell (Eric Arthur Blair) 1903 – 1980; English novelist, & author of the novel Nineteen Eighty-Four (1949).

You can have a spiritual awakening and discover a new side of you at any age. And best of all, love can happen at any age. Life can just start to get exciting when you're in your 40s and 50s. You have to believe that.
- Salma Hayek 1966 - ; Mexican American actress, director, & producer.

A major advantage of age is learning to accept people without passing judgment.
- Liz Carpenter 1920 – 2010; American writer, feminist, media advisor, speechwriter, & humorist.

No man was ever so completely skilled in the conduct of life, as not to receive new information from age and experience.
- Jonathan Swift 1667 – 1745; Irish essayist, satirist, poet, & cleric.

Diligent youth makes easy age.
(If you live your youth years diligently, it will save you from regret when you are old. That is, you take care of your health and do things you like that virtually only young people can do.)
– French Proverb (similar to the English version found in volume III)

The mind that is wise mourns less for what age takes away; than what it leaves behind.
- William Wordsworth 1770 – 1850; English Romantic poet.

When superstition is allowed to perform the task of old age in dulling the human temperament, we can say goodbye to all excellence in poetry, in painting, and in music.
- Denis Diderot 1713 – 1784; French philosopher, critic, & writer.

I'm inspired by people who keep on rolling, no matter their age.
- Jimmy Buffett 1946 - ; American singer-songwriter, author, actor, writer, & businessman.

There are people whose watch stops at a certain hour and who remain permanently at that age.
- Helen Rowland 1875 – 1950; American journalist, & humorist.

I will never be an old man. To me, old age is always 15 years older than I am.
- Francis Bacon 1561 – 1626; English philosopher, statesman, scientist, orator, & author.

Youth is wasted on the young.
(Youthful people lack common sense and wisdom, old people lack virility.)
– French Proverb

He is so old that his blood type was discontinued.
- Bill Dana 1924 - ; American comedian, actor, & screenwriter.

Not even old age knows how to love death.
- Sophocles 497 BC – 405 BC; Ancient Greek playwright.

Youth has no age.
- Pablo Picasso 1881 – 1973; Spanish artist, painter, sculptor, ceramicist, & printmaker.

Aging is not lost youth but a new stage of opportunity and strength.
- Betty Friedan 1921 – 2006; American writer, activist, feminist.

~Attitude~

The way a person views something or tends to behave towards it, often in an evaluative way. – **Definition of Attitude.**

Your attitude, not your aptitude, will determine your altitude.
- Zig Ziglar 1926 – 2012; American author & motivational speaker.

We are what our thoughts have made us; so take care about what you think. Words are secondary. Thoughts live; they travel far.
- Swami Vivekananda 1863 – 1902; Indian Hindu monk.

How do we keep our inner fire alive? Two things, at minimum, are needed: an ability to appreciate the positives in our life - and a commitment to action.
- Nathaniel Branden (Nathan Blumenthal) 1930 - ; Canadian psychotherapist & writer.

Act enthusiastic and you will be enthusiastic.
- Dale Carnegie 1888 – 1955; American writer, lecturer, & self-improvement coach.

Optimism may sometimes be delusional, but pessimism is always delusional.
- Alan Cohen 1954 - ; American businessman.

You're never a loser until you quit trying.
- Mike Ditka 1939 - ; American former NFL player, coach, & TV commentator.

That which doesn't kill us makes us stronger.
- Friedrich Nietzsche 1844 – 1900; German philosopher, philologist, critic, poet, & composer.

Don't wish it were easier, wish you were better.
- Jim Rohn 1930 – 2009; American entrepreneur, author, & motivational speaker.

Everything can be taken from a man but...the last of the human freedoms - to choose one's attitude in any given set of circumstances, to choose one's own way.
- Viktor E. Frankl 1905 – 1997; Austrian neurologist & psychiatrist.

Make sure your worst enemy doesn't live between your own two ears.
- Laird Hamilton 1964 - ; American surfer, model, & businessman.

Nature that framed us of four elements, warring within our breasts for regiment, doth teach us all to have aspiring minds.
- Niccolo Machiavelli 1469 – 1527; Italian historian, politician, diplomat, philosopher, & writer.

We cannot tell what may happen to us in the strange medley of life. But we can decide what happens in us—how we can take it, what we do with it —and that is what really counts in the end.
- Joseph Fort Newton 1876 – 1950; Minister, priest, & author.

If you're going through hell, keep going.
- Sir Winston Churchill 1874 – 1965; British Prime Minister 1940-1945 & 1951-1955, historian, artist, & Nobel Prize winner in literature.

Experience is not what happens to you - it's how you interpret what happens to you.
- Aldous Huxley 1894 – 1963; English writer.

Never leave that till tomorrow which you can do today.

- Benjamin Franklin 1706 – 1790; American politician, One of the founding fathers of the U.S., polymath, author, postmaster, scientist, musician, inventor, statesmen, critic, & diplomat.

To solve any problem, here are three questions to ask yourself: First, what could I do? Second, what could I read? And third, who could I ask?

- Jim Rohn 1930 – 2009; American entrepreneur, author, & motivational speaker.

You may not be responsible for getting knocked down, but you're certainly responsible for getting back up.

- Jesse Louis Jackson, Sr. (Jesse Louis Burns) 1941 - ; American civil rights activist & minister.

Though no one can go back and make a brand new start, anyone can start from now and make a brand new ending.

- Carl Bard (Carl Sandburg) 1878 – 1967; American writer, editor, & 3 time Pulitzer Prize winner.

I am not a product of my circumstances. I am a product of my decisions.

- Stephen Covey 1932 – 2012; American educator, author, businessman, lecturer & professor.

A pessimist sees the difficulty in every opportunity; an optimist sees the opportunity in every difficulty.

- Sir Winston Churchill 1874 – 1965; British Prime Minister 1940-1945 & 1951-1955, historian, artist, & Nobel Prize winner in literature.

Opportunities multiply as they are seized.

- Sun Tzu 544 BC – 496 BC; Chinese military general, strategist, & philosopher.

~Attitude~

Whether you think you can or you think you can't, you're right.
- Henry Ford 1863 – 1947; American industrialist, founder of the Ford Motor Company, & developer of the assembly line.

Let the refining and improving of your own life keep you so busy that you have little time to criticize others.
-H. Jackson Brown, Jr.; American author.

It is your decisions not your conditions that truly shape the quality of your life.
- Anthony Robbins 1960 - ; American self-help author, life coach, & motivational speaker.

You've got to take the initiative and play your game. In a decisive set, confidence is the difference.
- Chris Evert-Lloyd 1954 - ; American former top women's professional Tennis player.

Positive thinking will let you do everything better than negative thinking will.
- Zig Ziglar 1926 – 2012; American author & motivational speaker.

My motto was always to keep swinging. Whether I was in a slump or feeling badly or having trouble off the field, the only thing to do was keep swinging.
- Hank Aaron (Henry Louis "Hank" Aaron 1934 - ; American former top MLB player & Presidential Medal of Freedom award winner.

For myself I am an optimist - it does not seem to be much use being anything else.
- Sir Winston Churchill 1874 – 1965; British Prime Minister 1940-1945 & 1951-1955, historian, artist, & Nobel Prize winner in literature.

What is opportunity, and when does it knock? It never knocks. You can wait a whole lifetime, listening, hoping, and you will hear no knocking. None at all. You are opportunity, and you must knock on the door leading to your destiny.
- Maxwell Malts 1889 – 1975; American cosmetic surgeon & author.

As you put into practice the qualities of patience, punctuality, sincerity, and solicitude, you will have a better opinion of the world around you.
- Grenville Kleiser 1868-1935; Canadian author.

A devil is a mental attitude born out of false pride and self –exalting lies.
- Jabir Herbert Muhammad 1929 – 2008; businessmen & Muhammad Ali's manager.

They can because they think they can.
- Virgil (Publius Vergilius Maro 70 BC – 19 BC; Ancient Roman poet.

The future does not belong to those who are content with today, apathetic toward common problems and their fellow man alike, timid and fearful in the face of bold projects and new ideas. Rather, it will belong to those who can blend passion, reason and courage in a personal commitment to [their] ideals.
- Robert F. Kennedy 1925-1968; American politician & 64th Us Attorney General.

For success, attitude is equally as important as ability.
- Walter Scott 1771 – 1832; Scottish playwright, poet, & novelist.

10

You cannot control what happens to you, but you can control your attitude toward what happens to you, and in that, you will be mastering change rather than allowing it to master you.
- Brian Tracy 1944 - ; Canadian motivational speaker & author.

I ain't never been poor--just broke. Being poor is a state of mind; whereas, being broke is just a temporary situation.
- Mike Todd 1909 – 1958; American theater & film producer.

Ability is what you're capable of doing. Motivation determines what you do. Attitude determines how well you do it.
- Raymond Chandler 1888 – 1959; American British author & screenwriter.

Great effort springs naturally from great attitude.
- Pat Riley 1945 - ; American former basketball coach regarded as the one of the greatest coaches of all time.

Your attitude is like a box of crayons that color your world. Constantly color your picture gray, and your picture will always be bleak. Try adding some bright colors to the picture by including humor, and your picture begins to lighten up.
- Allen Klein 1931 – 2009; American businessman, talent agent, record label executive, & business manager.

Weakness of attitude becomes weakness of character.

- Albert Einstein 1879 – 1955; German American theoretical physicist, Nobel Prize winner, & developer of the general theory of relativity.

Albert Einstein 1879 – 1955; German American theoretical physicist, Nobel Prize winner, & developer of the general theory of relativity.
Known as the father of theoretical physics, he developed the theory of relativity, which governs one of the two main branches of physics. Einstein also helped persuade Roosevelt to develop the first atomic bomb but later in life deeply regretted that decision.

The way I see it, if you want the rainbow, you gotta put up with the rain.

- Dolly Parton 1946 - ; American singer-songwriter, Actress, Author, & philanthropist.

Keep your face always toward the sunshine - and shadows will fall behind you.

- Walt Whitman 1819 – 1892; American essayist, journalist, humanist & poet.

Nothing can dim the light which shines from within.

- Maya Angelou (Marguerite Ann Johnson) 1928 - ; American author & poet.

Take the attitude of a student, never be too big to ask questions, and never know too much to learn something new.
- Augustine "Og" Mandino II 1923 – 1996; American author.

Our attitude toward life determines life's attitude towards us.
- John N. Mitchell 1913 – 1988; American Attorney General of the United States.

Like success, failure is many things to many people. With Positive Mental Attitude, failure is a learning experience, a rung on the ladder, and a plateau at which to get your thoughts in order and prepare to try again.
- W. Clement Stone 1902 – 2002; American self-help author, businessman, & philanthropist.

Our environment, the world in which we live and work, is a mirror of our attitudes and expectations.
- Earl Nightingale 1921 – 1989; American author, motivational speaker, & radio personality.

My attitude is, do as much as I can while I'm free. And if I'm arrested I'll still do as much as I can.
- Aung San Suu Kyi 1945 - ; Burmese politician. Nobel Peace Prize, Congressional Gold Medal, & Presidential Medal of Freedom recipient.

If you have a positive attitude and constantly strive to give your best effort, eventually you will overcome your immediate problems and find you are ready for greater challenges.
- Pat Riley 1945 - ; American former basketball coach regarded as the one of the greatest coaches of all time.

There is, to be sure, no evil without something good. (Every cloud has its silver lining.)
- Latin Proverb

Sales are contingent upon the attitude of the salesman - not the attitude of the prospect.
- W. Clement Stone 1902 – 2002; American self-help author, businessman, & philanthropist.

Some people want it to happen, some wish it would happen, others make it happen.
- Michael Jordan 1963 - ; American former NBA player, entrepreneur, 6 times NBA champion, & 5 time MVP winner.

Little minds are tamed and subdued by misfortune; but great minds rise above them.
- Washington Irving 1783 – 1859; American author, essayist, biographer, historian, diplomat. Authored "The Legend of Sleepy Hollow" and "Rip Van Winkle".

And above all things, never think that you're not good enough yourself. A man should never think that. My belief is that in life people will take you at your own reckoning.
- Isaac Asimov (Isaak Yudovich Ozimov) 1920 – 1992; Russian American author & professor.

People like to look at their lives or their situation and say "It could be worse." A better mantra should be "It could be better."
- M.I. Seka – 1972 - ; Author & businessman.

When you have vision it affects your attitude. Your attitude is optimistic rather than pessimistic.
- Charles R. Swindoll 1934 - ; American pastor, author, educator, & radio personality.

~Attitude~

It is your attitude at the beginning of a task that determines success or failure. Don't let your pride or lack of courage stand in the way of saying you're sorry. Never stop doing your best just because someone doesn't give you credit.
It doesn't take strength to hold a grudge; it takes strength to let go of one.
I would rather make my name than inherit it.
- Unknown

The pessimist complains about the wind; the optimist expects it to change; the realist adjusts the sails.
- William Arthur Ward 1921 – 1994; American author.

Positive anything is better than negative nothing.
- Elbert Hubbard 1856-1915; American writer, philosopher, author, publisher, & artist.

A great attitude does much more than turn on the lights in our worlds; it seems to magically connect us to all sorts of serendipitous opportunities that were somehow absent before the change.
- Earl Nightingale 1921 – 1989; American author, motivational speaker, & radio personality.

Ingratitude is the essence of vileness.
- Immanuel Kant 1724 – 1804; German philosopher.

If you can't change your fate, change your attitude.
- Charles Revson 1906 – 1975; American businessman & philanthropist.

If Infinite striving to be the best is man's duty; it is its own reward.
- Mahatma Gandhi (Mohandas Karamchand Gandhi) 1869 – 1948; Indian leader of Indian nationalism that used non-violent civil disobedience to lead to Indian independence.

~Change~

~Change~

It is not the strongest of the species who survive, not the most intelligent, but those who are the most adaptive to change.

- Charles Darwin 1809 – 1882; English geologist, naturalist, author of "On the Origin of Species" which contributed greatly to the fact of evolution.

Charles Darwin 1809 – 1882: English geologist, naturalist, and author of "On the Origin of Species", which contributed greatly to the fact of evolution. *Even as a young man, Darwin was a gifted and passionate scientist. His research on evolution brought him to the conclusion that all life on our planet descended from common ancestors. From there natural selection took affect using a branching pattern based on the needs of the species given its environment. His research is the basis of all the life sciences explaining the diversity of life. Darwin's work has been one of the most influential in human history.*

When you're finished changing, you're finished.
- Benjamin Franklin 1706 – 1790; American politician, One of the founding fathers of the U.S., polymath, author, postmaster, scientist, musician, inventor, statesmen, critic, & diplomat.

It takes more courage to alter an opinion than to stick with it.
- Georg Christoph Lichtenberg 1742 – 1799; German scientist, & satirist.

You will never change your life until you change something you do daily.
- Mike Murdock 1946 - ; American televangelist & pastor.

The one who adapts his policy to the times prospers, and likewise that the one whose policy clashes with the demands of the times does not.
- Niccolo Machiavelli 1469 – 1527; Italian historian, politician, diplomat, philosopher, & writer.

You can never change things by fighting the existing reality. To change something, build a new model that makes the existing model obsolete.
- Richard Buckminster Fuller 1895 – 1983; American architect, author, theorist, inventor, designer, & futurist.

In our lives, change is unavoidable, loss is unavoidable. In the adaptability and ease with which we experience change, lies our happiness and freedom.
- Buddha (Gautama Buddha) 563 BCE – 483 BCE; Nepalese (present day) sage that taught principles that Buddhism was founded on.

To improve is to change; to be perfect is to change often.
- Sir Winston Churchill 1874 – 1965; British Prime Minister 1940-1945 & 1951-1955, historian, artist, & Nobel Prize winner in literature.

~Change~

Time is a sort of river of passing events, and strong is its current; no sooner is a thing brought to sight than it is swept by and another takes its place and this too will be swept away.
- Marcus Aurelius 121 AD – 180 AD; Roman Emperor & philosopher.

They must often change, who would be constant in happiness or wisdom.
- Confucius 551 BC – 479 BC; Chinese teacher, politician, & philosopher.

It's never too late to change the programming imprinted in childhood, carried in our genes or derived from previous lives; the solution is mindfulness in the present moment.
–Peter Shepherd 1952 - ; English Psychologist & author.

He is happy whose circumstances suit his temper; but he is more excellent who can suit his temper to any circumstances.
- David Hume 1711 – 1776; Scottish skeptic, philosopher, historian, economist, critic, & essayist.

What is necessary to change a person is to change his awareness of himself.
- Abraham H. Maslow 1908 – 1970; American psychologist & professor.

It is change, continuing change, inevitable change, that is the dominant factor in society today. No sensible decision can be made any longer without taking into account not only the world as it is, but the world as it will be.
- Isaac Asimov (Isaak Yudovich Ozimov) 1920 – 1992; Russian American author & professor.

~Change~

Life is a series of natural and spontaneous changes. Don't resist them, that only creates sorrow. Let things flow naturally forward in whatever way they like.
- Lao Tzu (Laozi) 6th century BC; Ancient Chinese philosopher.

We must all obey the great law of change. It is the most powerful law of nature.
- Edmund Burke 1729 – 1797; Irish statesman, author, & philosopher.

What I've experienced is that I can't know the future. I can't know if anything that I do will change what happens tomorrow. I can't know with certainty, but what I do know is if I do nothing, nothing will change.
- James Orbinski 1960 - ; English Canadian physician, writer, humanitarian, activist, & Nobel Peace Prize recipient.

When men are easy in their circumstances, they are naturally enemies to innovations.
- Joseph Addison 1672 – 1719; English poet, playwright, essayist, & politician.

A man who views the world the same at fifty as he did at twenty has wasted thirty years of his life.
- Muhammad Ali (Cassius Marcellus Clay, Jr.) 1942 - ; American Professional Boxing heavyweight champion known as the greatest boxer of the 20th century.

It takes a deep commitment to change and an even deeper commitment to grow.
- Ralph Ellison 1914 – 1994; American novelist, literary critic, & scholar.

~Communication & Relationship~

The real art of conversation is not only to say the right thing at the right time, but also to leave unsaid the wrong thing at the tempting moment.
- Lady Dorothy Nevill 1826 – 1913; English writer & plant collector.

A good listener is not only popular everywhere, but after a while he knows something.
- Wilson Mizner 1876 – 1933; American playwright. 1876 – 1933; American playwright.

With the gift of listening comes the gift of healing.
- Catherine Doherty (Elaterina Fyodorovna Kolyschkine de Hueck Doherty) 1896 – 1985; Russian author, social worker, & national speaker.

The best way to be boring is to leave nothing out.
- Voltaire (Francois-Marie Arouet) 1694 – 1778; French writer, historian, philosopher, & poet.

A smile is a curve that sets everything straight.
- Phyllis Diller 1917 – 2012; American actress & comedienne.

The expression a woman wears on her face is far more important than the clothes she wears on her back.
- Dale Carnegie 1888 – 1955; American writer, lecturer, & self-improvement coach.

Even the fool is thought wise if he remains silent.
- Swedish Proverb

As societies grow decadent, the language grows decadent, too. Words are used to disguise, not to illuminate, action: you liberate a city by destroying it. Words are to confuse, so that at election time people will solemnly vote against their own interests.
- Gore Vidal 1925 – 2012; American writer, critic, & humorist.

Women are never disarmed by compliments. Men always are. That is the difference between the sexes.
- Oscar Wilde 1854 – 1900; Irish writer, poet, & playwright.

Words have the power to both destroy and heal. When words are both true and kind, they can change our world.
- Buddha (Gautama Buddha) 563 BCE – 483 BCE; Nepalese (present day) sage that taught principles that Buddhism was founded on.

He that speaks much is much mistaken.
- Benjamin Franklin 1706 – 1790; American politician, One of the founding fathers of the U.S., polymath, author, postmaster, scientist, musician, inventor, statesmen, critic, & diplomat.

The first condition of progress is the removal of censorship.
- George Bernard Shaw 1856 – 1950; Irish playwright, co-founder of London School of Economics, critic, journalist, Nobel Prize winner, & Oscar winner.

Better to remain silent and be thought a fool than to speak out and remove all doubt.
- Abraham Lincoln 1809 – 1865; American politician, 16th President of the U.S. during the American Civil war & instrumental in abolishing slavery.

~Communication & Relationship~

He who speaks well lies well. He who stays quiet consents. He who whispers lies.
- Swedish Proverb

Rhetoric (effective use of language) is the art of ruling the minds of men.
- Plato 428 BC – 347 BC; Greek philosopher, mathematician, founder of Academy of Athens (the first institute of higher learning), student of Socrates & teacher of Aristotle.

Too often the strong, silent man is silent only because he does not know what to say, and is reputed strong only because he has remained silent.
- Sir Winston Churchill 1874 – 1965; British Prime Minister 1940-1945 & 1951-1955, historian, artist, & Nobel Prize winner in literature.

When you're young, you look at most of the programs on television and think, 'There's a conspiracy! The networks have conspired to dumb us down!' But when you get a little older, you realize that's not true. The networks are in the business to make money by giving people exactly what they want. That's a far more depressing thought. Conspiracy is optimistic. You can shoot the bastards! We can have a revolution!
- Steve Jobs 1955 – 2011; American inventor, entrepreneur, marketer, & co-founder of Apple Inc.

Tact is the ability to describe others as they see themselves.
- Abraham Lincoln 1809 – 1865; American politician, 16th President of the U.S. during the American Civil war & instrumental in abolishing slavery.

The best makeup is a smile. The best jewelry is modesty. The best clothing is confidence.
- Unknown

Silence is a true friend who never betrays.
- *Confucius 551 BC – 479 BC; Chinese teacher, politician, & philosopher.*

There is some pleasure even in words, when they bring forgetfulness of present miseries.
- *Sophocles 497 BC – 405 BC; Ancient Greek playwright.*

If you have an important point to make, don't try to be subtle or clever. Use a pile driver. Hit the point once. Then come back and hit it again. Then hit it a third time - a tremendous whack.
- *Sir Winston Churchill 1874 – 1965; British Prime Minister 1940-1945 & 1951-1955, historian, artist, & Nobel Prize winner in literature.*

Wise men talk because they have something to say; fools talk because they have to say something.
- *Plato 428 BC – 347 BC; Greek philosopher, mathematician, founder of Academy of Athens (the first institute of higher learning), student of Socrates & teacher of Aristotle.*

When we focus on clarifying what is being observed, felt, and needed rather than on diagnosing and judging, we discover the depth of our own compassion.
- *Marshall Rosenberg 1934 - ; American psychologist.*

Character may almost be called the most effective means of persuasion.
- *Aristotle 384 BC – 322 BC; Greek philosopher, polymath, & one of the fathers of Western philosophy.*

As the age of television progresses the Reagans will be the rule, not the exception. To be perfect for television is all a President has to be these days.
- *Gore Vidal 1925 – 2012; American writer, critic, & humorist.*

Now I see that going out into the testing ground of men it is the tongue and not the deed that wins the day.

- Sophocles 497 BC – 405 BC; Ancient Greek playwright.

Sophocles 497 BC – 405 BC: Ancient Greek playwright. *Believed to have written 123 plays during his lifetime with only 7 surviving in complete form. Sophocles was the preeminent playwright for almost 50 years winning many of the competitions at the time. He is also known for adding a third actor in plays to reduce the role of the chorus, add deeper character development, and increased conflict. He's also known for introducing background scenery.*

When marrying, ask yourself this question: Do you believe that you will be able to converse well with this person into your old age? Everything else in marriage is transitory.

- Friedrich Nietzsche 1844 – 1900; German philosopher, philologist, critic, poet, & composer.

It is not one person's fault if two people quarrel. (It takes two to make a quarrel.)
- Swedish Proverb

The true secret of giving advice is, after you have honestly given it, to be perfectly indifferent whether it is taken or not, and never persist in trying to set people right.

- *Henry Ward Beecher 1813-1887; American clergymen, speaker, & abolitionist.*

Don't you know that silence supports the accuser's charge?

- *Sophocles 497 BC – 405 BC; Ancient Greek playwright.*

~Communication & Relationship~

~Courage & Fear~

None but the brave deserve the fair. (Only the courageous deserve the finer things in life.)
- English Proverb

Most of us have far more courage than we ever dreamed we possessed.
- Dale Carnegie 1888 – 1955; American writer, lecturer, & self-improvement coach.

Fix reason firmly in her seat, and call to her tribunal every fact, every opinion. Question with boldness even the existence of a God; because, if there be one, he must more approve of the homage of reason, than that of blindfolded fear.
- Thomas Jefferson 1743 – 1826; One of the founding fathers of U.S., the principal author of the Declaration of Independence, & 3rd president of U.S.

The first quality that is needed is audacity.
- Sir Winston Churchill 1874 – 1965; British Prime Minister 1940-1945 & 1951-1955, historian, artist, & Nobel Prize winner in literature.

Evil (ignorance) is like a shadow—it has no real substance of its own, it is simply a lack of light. You cannot cause a shadow to disappear by trying to fight it, stamp on it, by railing against it, or any other form of emotional or physical resistance. In order to cause a shadow to disappear, you must shine light on it.
- Shakti Gawain (Carol Louisa Gawain) 1948 - ; American new age author.

With the fearful strain that is on me night and day, if I did not laugh I should die.
- Abraham Lincoln 1809 – 1865; 16th President of the U.S. during the American Civil war, instrumental in abolishing slavery.

He who is not courageous enough to take risks will accomplish nothing in life.
- Muhammad Ali (Cassius Marcellus Clay, Jr.) 1942 - ; American Professional Boxing heavyweight champion known as the greatest boxer of the 20th century.

Muhammad Ali (Cassius Marcellus Clay, Jr.) 1942 – Present: American Professional Boxing heavyweight champion known as the greatest boxer of the 20th century. *Besides his boxing career, Ali was also famous for his values of freedom, justice, and equality. 3 years after winning the heavyweight title, Ali refused to be drafted into the military to fight in the Vietnam War. He was subsequently arrested, found guilty, and stripped of his title. Ali did not fight again until the U.S. Supreme court overturned his conviction, 4 years later in 1971. During his time away from boxing, Ali spoke publically in opposition to the Vietnam War, advocated American pride and social/racial justice.*

Because fear is insatiable, everything that is insatiable is born of fear.
- Alan Cohen 1954 - ; American businessman.

Faced with what is right, to leave it undone shows a lack of courage.

- Confucius 551 BC – 479 BC; Chinese teacher, politician, & philosopher.

Courage lost, all lost (Without courage, there is nothing.)

- Dutch Proverb

You can conquer almost any fear if you will only make up your mind to do so. For remember, fear doesn't exist anywhere except in the mind.

- Dale Carnegie 1888 – 1955; American writer, lecturer, & self-improvement coach.

He, who fears he will suffer, already suffers from his fear.

- Michel de Montaigne 1533 – 1592; French Essayist & influential author.

A coward is much more exposed to quarrels than a man of spirit.

- Thomas Jefferson 1743 – 1826; One of the founding fathers of U.S., the principal author of the Declaration of Independence, & 3rd president of U.S.

A word does not frighten the man who, in acting, feels no fear.

- Sophocles 497 BC – 405 BC; Ancient Greek playwright.

If you don't stand for something, you'll fall for anything.

- Dr. Martin Luther King, Jr. (Michael King) 1929 - 1968; American clergyman, minister, civil rights activist. Nobel Peace Prize, Presidential Medal of Freedom, & Congressional Gold Medal recipient.

Conviction is worthless unless it is converted into conduct.

-Thomas Carlyle 1795 – 1881; Scottish philosopher, writer, historian, essayist, satirist, & teacher.

Physical bravery is an animal instinct; moral bravery is much higher and truer courage.
- Wendell Phillips 1811-1884; American abolitionist, lawyer, & orator.

The ultimate measure of man is not where he stands in moments of comfort and convenience, but where he stands at times of challenge and controversy.
- Dr. Martin Luther King, Jr. (Michael King) 1929 - 1968; American clergyman, minister, civil rights activist. Nobel Peace Prize, Presidential Medal of Freedom, & Congressional Gold Medal recipient.

Anyone who has never made a mistake has never tried anything new.
- Albert Einstein 1879 – 1955; German American theoretical physicist, Nobel Prize winner, & developer of the general theory of relativity.

To see the right and not to do it is cowardice.
- Confucius 551 BC – 479 BC; Chinese teacher, politician, & philosopher.

Nothing in life is to be feared. It is only to be understood.
- Marie S. Curie 1867 – 1934; Polish physicist, chemist, & Nobel Prize recipient.

Never let the fear of striking out get in your way.
- Babe Ruth 1895 – 1948; American professional baseball player.

It takes courage to grow up and turn out to be who you really are.
- e.e. (Edward Estlin) Cummings 1894 – 1962; American poet, painter, essayist, author, & playwright.

~Courage & Fear~

What we fear doing most is usually what we most need to do.
- Tim Ferriss 1977 - ; American author & speaker.

A moment of choice is a moment of truth. It's the testing point of our character and competence.
- Stephen Covey 1932 – 2012; American educator, author, businessman, lecturer & professor.

It is our choices that show what we truly are, far more than our abilities.
- J.K. Rowling (Joanne Rowling) 1965 - ; English author of "The Harry Potter" series.

I'm not afraid... I was BORN for this!
- Joan of Arc 1412 – 1431; French folk heroine & patron saint of France.

To be yourself in a world that is constantly trying to make you something else is the greatest accomplishment.
- Ralph Waldo Emerson 1803-1882; American lecturer, poet, & essayist.

Too many people overvalue what they are not and undervalue what they are.
- Malcolm Forbes 1919 – 1990; American publisher of Forbes magazine.

People who consider themselves victims of their circumstances will always remain victims unless they develop a greater vision for their lives.
- Stedman Graham 1951 - ; American businessman, author, speaker & educator.

Fall seven times, stand up eight.
- Japanese Proverb

Toil and risk are the price of glory, but it is a lovely thing to live with courage and die leaving an everlasting fame.

- Alexander the Great (Alexander III of Macedon) 356 BC – 323 BC; was a king of Macedon, a state in northern ancient Greece. By age 30 conquered an empire from the Mediterranean to the Himalayans.

Alexander the Great (Alexander III of Macedon) 356 BC – 323 BC: was a king of Macedon, a state in northern ancient Greece. By the age of 30 Alexander conquered an empire from the Mediterranean to the Himalayans (Modern day Pakistan). *Tutored by Aristotle, Alexander successfully succeeded his father Philip II of Macedon to the throne after his assassination. Taking control of a strong kingdom and an experienced army, Alexander began consolidating his power and expanding his kingdom. Seeking to reach the end of the world he started a campaign that ended in India before his troops demanded they turn back. Undefeated in battle, he is considered one of the most successful military commanders in history.*

One of the greatest discoveries a man makes, one of his great surprises, is to find he can do what he was afraid he couldn't do.

- Henry Ford 1863 – 1947; American industrialist, founder of the Ford Motor Company, & developer of the assembly line.

~Courage & Fear~

For it is not death or hardship that is a fearful thing, but the fear of death or hardship.
- Epictetus 55-135; Ancient Greek sage & philosopher.

You may never know what results will come from your actions, but if you do nothing - there will be no results.
- Mahatma Gandhi (Mohandas Karamchand Gandhi) 1869 – 1948; Indian leader of Indian nationalism that used non-violent civil disobedience to lead to Indian independence.

People grow through experience if they meet life honestly and courageously. This is how character is built.
- Anna Eleanor Roosevelt 1884 – 1962; Wife of Franklin D. Roosevelt, diplomat, human rights activist, first lady of the U.S. from 1933 to 1945.

Courage is the price that life exacts for granting peace.
- Amelia Earhart 1897 – 1937; American aviator & author.

It is curious that physical courage should be so common in the world and moral courage so rare.
- Mark Twain (Samuel Langhorne Clemens) 1835-1910; American author & humorist.

Courage is the ladder on which all the other virtues mount.
- Brandan Francis Behan 1923-1964; Irish poet, novelist, writer, & playwright.

He who passively accepts evil is as much involved in it as he who helps to perpetrate it. He who accepts evil without protesting against it is really cooperating with it.
- Dr. Martin Luther King, Jr. (Michael King) 1929 - 1968; American clergyman, minister, civil rights activist. Nobel Peace Prize, Presidential Medal of Freedom, & Congressional Gold Medal recipient.

You may have to fight a battle more than once to win it.
- Margaret Thatcher 1925 – 2013; English politician & Prime Minister.

What would life be if we had no courage to attempt anything?
- Vincent Van Gogh 1853-1890; Dutch painter.

It's not the size of the dog in the fight; it's the size of the fight in the dog.
- Mark Twain (Samuel Langhorne Clemens) 1835-1910; American author & humorist.

Mark Twain (Samuel Langhorne Clemens) 1835-1910; American author & humorist. *Most noted for his sharp wit, satire, and popular speeches. Twain is also known for writing the great American novels The Adventures of Tom Sawyer in 1876 and, its sequel, The Adventures of Huckleberry Finn in 1885. An Adamant supporter of abolition, women's rights, and civil rights. Twain died of a heart attack in 1910.*

A coward gets scared and quits. A hero gets scared, but still goes on.
It is easy to do right out of fear, but it is better to do right because right is right.
- Louis Farrakhan Muhammad, Sr. (Louis Eugene Wolcott) 1933 - ; American leader of the Nation of Islam.

Man cannot discover new oceans unless he has the courage to lose sight of the shore.
- André Gide 1869-1951; French author & Nobel Prize winner in literature.

A man can be as great as he wants to be. If you believe in yourself and have the courage, the determination, the dedication, the competitive drive and if you are willing to sacrifice the little things in life and pay the price for the things that are worthwhile, it can be done.
- Vince Lombardi 1913 – 1970; American football player, & coach.

~Criticism~

To silence criticism is to silence freedom.
- Sidney Hook 1902 – 1989; American philosopher.

It doesn't matter if a cat is black or white, so long as it catches mice.
- Deng Xiaoping 1904 – 1997; Chinese politician & reformer.

It is the nature of the artist to mind excessively what is said about him. Literature is strewn with the wreckage of men who have minded beyond reason the opinions of others.
- Virginia Woolf 1882 – 1941; English writer.

Dare to risk public criticism.
- Mary Kay Ash 1918 – 2001; American entrepreneur & founder of Mary Kay Cosmetics.

When I am abroad, I always make it a rule never to criticize or attack the government of my own country. I make up for lost time when I come home.
- Sir Winston Churchill 1874 – 1965; British Prime Minister 1940-1945 & 1951-1955, historian, artist, & Nobel Prize winner in literature.

Your time is limited, so don't waste it living someone else's life and don't let the noise of others' opinions drown out your own inner voice. Most important, have the courage to follow your heart and intuition. They somehow already know what you truly want to become.
- Steve Jobs 1955 – 2011; American inventor, entrepreneur, marketer, & co-founder of Apple Inc.

The public is the only critic whose opinion is worth anything at all.
- Mark Twain (Samuel Langhorne Clemens) 1835-1910; American author & humorist.

Every person who has mastered a profession is a skeptic concerning it.
- George Bernard Shaw 1856 – 1950; Irish playwright, co-founder of London School of Economics, critic, journalist, Nobel Prize winner, & Oscar winner

The dread of criticism is the death of genius.
-William Gilmore Simms 1806 – 1870; American poet, novelist, & historian.

What is in question is a kind of book reviewing which seems to be more and more popular: the loose putting down of opinions as though they were facts, and the treating of facts as though they were opinions.
- Gore Vidal 1925 – 2012; American writer, critic, & humorist.

~Death~

Our dead are never dead to us, until we have forgotten them.
- George Eliot (Mary Anne Evans) 1819 – 1880; English novelist.

Death is a horrible experience for the living.
- M.I. Seka 1972 - ; Author & businessman.

No one knows whether death, which people fear to be the greatest evil, may not be the greatest good.
- Plato 428 BC – 347 BC; Greek philosopher, mathematician, founder of Academy of Athens (the first institute of higher learning), student of Socrates & teacher of Aristotle.

I look upon death to be as necessary to our constitution as sleep. We shall rise refreshed in the morning.
- Benjamin Franklin 1706 – 1790; American politician, One of the founding fathers of the U.S., polymath, author, postmaster, scientist, musician, inventor, statesmen, critic, & diplomat.

The life of the dead is placed in the memory of the living.
- Marcus Tullius Cicero 106 BC – 43BC; Roman philosopher, politician, lawyer, orator, political theorist, consul, & constitutionalist.

I've told my children that when I die, to release balloons in the sky to celebrate that I graduated. For me, death is a graduation.
- Elisabeth Kubler-Ross 1926 – 2004; Swiss American psychiatrist.

Martyrdom: The only way a man can become famous without ability.
- George Bernard Shaw 1856 – 1950; Irish playwright, co-founder of London School of Economics, critic, journalist, Nobel Prize winner, & Oscar winner.

38

Death doesn't fear people.
- Spanish Proverb

Without death there would be very little progress.
- Steve Jobs 1955 – 2011; American inventor, entrepreneur, marketer, & co-founder of Apple Inc.

Death is the wake-up call, the unavoidable mandate, the makes enlightenment possible, and helps our souls to grow. This is why when asked on his deathbed for one final word of advice, responded to his pupils, "Practice dying."
- Plato 428 BC – 347 BC; Greek philosopher, mathematician, founder of Academy of Athens (the first institute of higher learning), student of Socrates & teacher of Aristotle.

When I look back on all these worries, I remember the story of the old man who said on his deathbed that he had had a lot of trouble in his life, most of which had never happened.
- Sir Winston Churchill 1874 – 1965; British Prime Minister 1940-1945 & 1951-1955, historian, artist, Nobel Prize winner in literature.

The patient is not likely to recover who makes the doctor his heir.
- Thomas Fuller 1608 – 1661; English historian & writer.

Most people would sooner die than think; in fact they do so.
- Bertrand Russell 1872 – 1970; English philosopher, logician, mathematician, historian, critic, & Nobel Prize in Literature recipient.

After I'm dead I'd rather have people ask why I have no monument than why I have one.
- Cato the Elder 234 BC – 149 BC; Ancient Roman statesman.

The death of one, the bread of the other.
(One person often prospers from the misfortune of another.)
- *Swedish Proverb*

Let us live so that when we come to die even the undertaker will be sorry.
- *Mark Twain (Samuel Langhorne Clemens) 1835-1910; American author & humorist.*

Remember that you are going to die. (Latin equivalent: Memento mori. You won't live forever, so make sure you do things which are really entertaining or really important.)
- *German Proverb*

~Dreams & Imagination~

The best way to make your dreams come true is to wake up.
- Paul Valery 1871 – 1945; French poet, essayist, & philosopher.

We are what we imagine. Our very existence consists in our imagination of ourselves. The greatest tragedy that can befall us is to go unimagined.
- N. Scott Momaday 1934 - ; Native American author & Pulitzer Prize recipient.

Nothing ever goes away until it has taught us what we need to know.
- Pema Chodron (Deirdre Blomfield-Brown) 1936 - ; American author, teacher, & ordained nun in Tibetan Buddhism.

The human race is governed by its imagination.
- Napoleon Bonaparte 1769 – 1821; French Emperor, military & political leader.

Too many of us are not living our dreams because we are living our fears.
- Les Brown 1945 - ; American motivational speaker, politician, author, & TV host.

Great dreams of great dreamers are always transcended.
- Abdul Kalam 1931; Indian scientist, & 11th president of India.

To accomplish great things, we must not only act, but also dream, not only plan, but also believe.
- Anatole France 1844 – 1924; French journalist, poet, author, & Nobel Prize in Literature recipient.

What we think, we become.

- Buddha (Gautama Buddha) 563 BCE – 483 BCE; Nepalese (present day) sage that taught principles that Buddhism was founded on.

If you want to reach a goal, you must 'see the reaching' in your own mind before you actually arrive at your goal.

- Zig Ziglar 1926 – 2012; American author & motivational speaker.

Whatever you can do, or dream you can, begin it. Boldness has genius, power and magic in it.

– Johann Wolfang Von Goethe 1749 – 1832; German writer & politician.

The greatest danger for most of us is not that our aim is too high and we miss it, but that it is too low and we reach it.

- Michelangelo (Michelangelo di Lodovico Buonarroti Simoni) 1475 – 1564; Italian sculptor, painter, architect, poet, & engineer.

A man is not a man until he is able and willing to accept his own vision of the world, no matter how radically this vision departs from that of others.

- James A. Baldwin 1924 – 1987; American playwright, novelist, essayist, poet, critic, & civil rights activist.

Be careful what you water your dreams with. Water them with worry and fear and you will produce weeds that choke the life from your dream. Water them with optimism and solutions and you will cultivate success.

- Lao Tzu 6th century BC; Chinese philosopher.

~Dreams & Imagination~

To understand the heart and mind of a person, look not at what he has already achieved, but at what he aspires to.
- *Khalil Gibran 1883 – 1931; Lebanese artist, poet, & writer.*

Every great dream begins with a dreamer. Always remember, you have within you the strength, the patience, and the passion to reach for the stars to change the world.
- *Harriet Tubman (Araminta Harriet Ross) 1820 – 1913; African American slave, abolitionist, humanitarian, union spy, & woman's rights activist.*

An athlete cannot run with money in his pockets. He must run with hope in his heart and dreams in his head.
- *Emil Zatopek 1922 – 2000; Czech long distance runner & Olympic gold medal winner.*

When I woke up this morning my girlfriend asked me, 'Did you sleep well?' I said 'No, I made a few mistakes.'
- *Steven Wright 1955 - ; American Comedian, actor, & writer.*

Whatever the mind of man can conceive and believe, it can achieve.
- *Napoleon Hill 1883 – 1970; American author on motivation.*

The problems of the world cannot possibly be solved by skeptics or cynics whose horizons are limited by the obvious realities. We need men who can dream of things that never were.
- *John F. Kennedy 1917-1963; American politician & 35th President of the U.S.*

In my wildest dreams, I could not have imagined a sweeter life.
– *Hugh Hefner 1925 - ; American magazine publisher & founder of Playboy magazine.*

~Dreams & Imagination~

Trust in dreams, for in them is hidden the gate to eternity.
- Khalil Gibran 1883 – 1931; Lebanese artist, poet, & writer.

Khalil Gibran 1883 – 1931: Lebanese artist, poet, & writer. *Gibran immigrated to the U.S. to study art and to begin his literary career. In the West he is largely known by his book "The Prophet" published in 1923. Gibran died in New York but was eventually moved to Lebanon for burial. He has monuments in Boston, Washington D.C., and Lebanon.*

Definiteness of purpose is the starting point of all achievement.
- W. Clement Stone 1902 – 2002; American self-help author, businessman, & philanthropist.

All men dream, but not equally. Those who dream by night in the dusty recesses of their minds, wake in the day to find that it was vanity: but the dreamers of the day are dangerous men, for they may act on their dreams with open eyes, to make them possible.
- T. E. (Thomas Edward) Lawrence 1888 – 1935; English army officer, author, & known as "Lawrence of Arabia".

To believe in yourself and to follow your dreams, to have goals in life and a drive to succeed, and to surround yourself with the things and the people that make you happy - this is success!

- Sasha Azevedo 1978 - ; Actress.

~Environment & Nature~

It is horrifying that we have to fight our own government to save the environment.
- Ansel Adams 1902 – 1984; American photographer & environmentalist.

Nature and books belong to the eyes that see them.
- Ralph Waldo Emerson 1803-1882; American lecturer, poet, & essayist.

Our nature is the mind. And the mind is our nature.
- Bodhidharma 5th century CE; Chinese, Persian, or Indian Buddhist monk credited with bringing Ch'an (a form of Buddhisim) to China.

Nature never deceives us; it is we who deceive ourselves.
- Jean-Jacques Rousseau 1712 – 1778; Genevan (currently Switzerland) writer, composer, & philosopher.

Self-preservation is the first law of nature.
- Samuel Butler 1835 – 1902; English author.

Loss is nothing else but change, and change is Nature's delight.
- Marcus Aurelius 121 AD – 180 AD; Roman Emperor & philosopher.

A radical inner transformation and rise to a new level of consciousness might be the only real hope we have in the current global crisis brought on by the dominance of the Western mechanistic paradigm.
- Stanislav Grof 1931 - ; Czech psychiatrist.

Water is the driving force of all nature.

- Leonardo da Vinci 1452 – 1519; Italian polymath, painter, sculptor, architect, musician, mathematician, engineer, inventor, geologist, anatomist, cartographer, & botanist.

In every walk with nature one receives far more than he seeks.

- John Muir 1838 – 1914; Scottish American naturalist, author, & conservationist.

To be admitted to Nature's hearth costs nothing. None is excluded, but excludes himself. You have only to push aside the curtain.

- Henry David Thoreau 1817-1862; American poet, philosopher, author, abolitionist, naturalist, surveyor, & historian.

Henry David Thoreau 1817-1862; American poet,philosopher, author, abolitionist, naturalist, surveyor, & historian. *Best known for his book "Walden" and his essay "Resistance to Civil Government" which influenced Gandhi, Dr. Martin Luther King Jr., and Leo Tolstoy. He was an anarchist who advocated for no government at all, but also spoke against cooperating with an unjust government.*

Nature has planted in our minds an insatiable longing to see the truth.

- Marcus Tullius Cicero 106 BC – 43BC; Roman philosopher, politician, lawyer, orator, political theorist, consul, & constitutionalist.

47

~Environment & Nature~

Forget not that the earth delights to feel your bare feet and the winds long to play with your hair.
- Khalil Gibran 1883 – 1931; Lebanese artist, poet, & writer.

Let everyone sweep in front of his own door, and the whole world will be clean.
– Johann Wolfang Von Goethe 1749 – 1832; German writer & politician.

We shape our buildings; thereafter they shape us.
- Sir Winston Churchill 1874 – 1965; British Prime Minister 1940-1945 & 1951-1955, historian, artist, & Nobel Prize winner in literature.

They are much to be pitied who have not been given a taste for nature early in life.
- Jane Austen 1775 – 1817; English novelist.

~Faith & Spirituality~

I do not feel obliged to believe that the same God who has endowed us with sense, reason, and intellect has intended us to forgo their use.
- Galileo Galilei 1564 – 1642; Italian physicist, mathematician, astronomer, & philosopher & polymath.

When I look upon seamen, men of science and philosophers, man is the wisest of all beings; when I look upon priests and prophets nothing is as contemptible as man.
- Diogenes of Sinope 404 BCE – 323 BCE; Ancient Greek philosopher.

It is possible that mankind is on the threshold of a golden age; but, if so, it will be necessary first to slay the dragon that guards the door, and this dragon is religion.
- Bertrand Russell 1872 – 1970; English philosopher, logician, mathematician, historian, critic, & Nobel Prize in Literature recipient.

Is it not a species of blasphemy to call the New Testament revealed religion, when we see in it such contradictions and absurdities?
- Thomas Paine 1737 – 1809; English-American author, political activist, theorist, & revolutionary.

There is not enough love and goodness in the world to permit giving any of it away to imaginary beings.
- Friedrich Nietzsche 1844 – 1900; German philosopher, philologist, critic, poet, & composer.

The Bible shows the way to go to heaven, not the way the heavens go.

- Galileo Galilei 1564 – 1642; Italian physicist, mathematician, astronomer, & philosopher & polymath.

Galileo Galilei 1564 – 1642: Italian physicist, mathematician, astronomer, philosopher & polymath. *One of the greatest scientific minds in history played a major role in improvements of the telescope, compasses, and advocated the idea of heliocentrism, which stated that the earth revolved around the sun. He has been called the father of modern observational astronomy, physics, science, and modern science. He was tried for heresy and spent the rest of his life under house arrest.*

What then do you call your soul? What idea have you of it? You cannot of yourselves, without revelation, admit the existence within you of anything but a power unknown to you of feeling and thinking.

- Voltaire (Francois-Marie Arouet) 1694 – 1778; French writer, historian, philosopher, & poet.

After coming into contact with a religious man I always feel I must wash my hands.

- Friedrich Nietzsche 1844 – 1900; German philosopher, philologist, critic, poet, & composer.

I have noticed even people who claim everything is predestined, and that we can do nothing to change it, look before they cross the road.

- Stephen Hawking 1942 - ; English theoretical physicist, cosmologist, author, Director of Research at University of Cambridge.

The way to silence religious disputes is to take no notice of them.

- Thomas Jefferson 1743 – 1826; One of the founding fathers of U.S., the principal author of the Declaration of Independence, & 3rd president of U.S.

My country is the world, and my religion is to do good.

- Thomas Paine 1737 – 1809; English-American author, political activist, theorist, & revolutionary.

The way to see by Faith is to shut the Eye of Reason.

- Benjamin Franklin 1706 – 1790; American politician, One of the founding fathers of the U.S., polymath, author, postmaster, scientist, musician, inventor, statesmen, critic, & diplomat.

When the gods wish to punish us they answer our prayers.

- Oscar Wilde 1854 – 1900; Irish writer, poet, & playwright.

No religion has mandated killing others as a requirement for its sustenance or promotion.

- Abdul Kalam 1931; Indian scientist, & 11th president of India.

It is folly for a man to pray to the gods for that which he has the power to obtain by himself.

- Epicurus 341 BC – 270 BC; Greek philosopher.

Faith is believing what you know ain't so.

- Mark Twain (Samuel Langhorne Clemens) 1835-1910; American author & humorist.

You pray in your distress and in your need; would that you might also pray in the fullness of your joy and in your days of abundance.
- Khalil Gibran 1883 – 1931; Lebanese artist, poet, & writer.

I'm halfway through Genesis and quite appalled by the disgraceful behavior of all the characters, including God.
- J.R. Ackerley 1896 – 1967; British writer & editor.

Every day people are straying away from the church and going back to God.
- Lenny Bruce (Leonard Alfred Schneider) 1925 – 1966; American Stand-up comedian, critic, & satirist.

My mind is my own church.
- Thomas Paine 1737 – 1809; English-American author, political activist, theorist, & revolutionary.

Religion is what keeps the poor from murdering the rich.
- Napoleon Bonaparte 1769 – 1821; French Emperor, military & political leader.

Christ died for our sins. Dare we make his martyrdom meaningless by not committing them?
- Jules Feiffer 1929 - ; American syndicated cartoonist & Pulitzer Prize winner.

Anyone who has the power to make you believe absurdities has the power to make you commit injustices.
- Voltaire (Francois-Marie Arouet) 1694 – 1778; French writer, historian, philosopher, & poet.

Trust in Allah, but tie your camel.
- Arabian proverb

Religions are many and diverse, but reason and goodness are one.
- Elbert Hubbard 1856-1915; American writer, philosopher, author, publisher, & artist.

~Faith & Spirituality~

The World is my country, all mankind are my brethren, and to do good is my religion.
- Thomas Paine 1737 – 1809; English-American author, political activist, theorist, & revolutionary.

Religion backed up by commerce is awful hard for a heathen to overcome.
- Will Rogers 1879 – 1935; American humorist, social commentator, actor, & writer.

He that humbles himself wishes to be exalted (elevated).
- Friedrich Nietzsche 1844 – 1900; German philosopher, philologist, critic, poet, & composer.

God could end misery in the world, but if he did, nobody would speak to him.
- Bill Maher 1956 - ; American stand-up comedian, TV host, political commentator, satirist, author, & actor.

Going to church no more makes you a Christian than standing in a garage makes you a car.
- William Ashley Sunday 1862 – 1935; American clergyman.

All that spirits desire, spirits attain.
- Khalil Gibran 1883 – 1931; Lebanese artist, poet, & writer.

Religion gives people hope in a world torn apart by religion.
- Jon Stewart (Jonathan Stuart Leibowitz) 1962 - ; American political satirist, writer, director, TV host, actor, media critic, stand-up comedian, & producer.

Everybody wants to go to heaven, but nobody wants to die.
- Joe Louis (Joseph Louis Barrow) 1914 – 1981; American professional boxing champion.

Men create the gods in their own image.
- Xenophanes 570 BC – 475 BC; Ancient Greek philosopher, theologian, poet, & critic.

~Faith & Spirituality~

Men create gods after their own image, not only with regard to their form but with regard to their mode of life.

- Aristotle 384 BC – 322 BC; Greek philosopher, polymath, & one of the fathers of Western philosophy.

Aristotle 384 BC – 322 BC: Greek philosopher, polymath, & one of the fathers of Western philosophy. *A pupil of Plato and teacher of Alexander the Great, his writings were one of the first to create a comprehensive system of Western Philosophy. Aristotle believed that people's perception of the world made up their concepts and knowledge. Aristotle's has contributed greatly to physics, the life sciences, and to ethics.*

When I think of all the harm the Bible has done, I despair of ever writing anything to equal it.

- Oscar Wilde 1854 – 1900; Irish writer, poet, & playwright.

If I can inspire one of these youngsters to develop the talent I know they possess, then my monument will be in their work.

- Augusta Savage 1892 – 1962; African American sculptor, teacher, & civil rights activist.

~Faith & Spirituality~

Life in Lubbock, Texas, taught me two things. One is that God loves you and you're going to burn in hell. The other is that sex is the most awful, filthy thing there is and you should save it for someone you love.
- Butch Hancock 1945 - ; American country/folk recording artist & song writer.

The Vatican is a dagger in the heart of Italy.
- Thomas Paine 1737 – 1809; English-American author, political activist, theorist, & revolutionary.

Unless you sin, Jesus died for nothing.
- Unknown

When God sneezed, I didn't know what to say.
- Henny Youngman 1906 – 1998; English American comedian.

We must no more ask whether the soul and body are one than ask whether the wax and the figure impressed on it are one.
- Aristotle 384 BC – 322 BC; Greek philosopher, polymath, & one of the fathers of Western philosophy.

Man was made at the end of the week's work when God was tired.
- Mark Twain (Samuel Langhorne Clemens) 1835-1910; American author & humorist.

Superstition is to religion what astrology is to astronomy the mad daughter of a wise mother. These daughters have too long dominated the earth.
- Voltaire (Francois-Marie Arouet) 1694 – 1778; French writer, historian, philosopher, & poet.

I cannot believe in a God who wants to be praised all the time.
- Friedrich Nietzsche 1844 – 1900; German philosopher, philologist, critic, poet, & composer.

Such as are your habitual thoughts, such also will be the character of your mind; for the soul is dyed by the thoughts.
- Marcus Aurelius 121 AD – 180 AD; Roman Emperor & philosopher.

Know in your heart that all things are possible. We couldn't conceive of a miracle if none had ever happened.
- Libbie Fudim ; Unknown.

It's not the religion that's the problem, it's the dogmatic, narrow and closed minded thinking that religion promotes, that's the problem.
- M.I. Seka 1972 - ; Author & businessman.

Organized religion is a sham and a crutch for weak-minded people who need strength in numbers. It tells people to go out and stick their noses in other people's business.
- Jesse Ventura (James George Janos) 1951 - ; American politician, actor, author, veteran, & former professional wrestler.

Science has proof without any certainty. Creationists have certainty without any proof.
- Ashley Montagu (Montaue Francis Ashley-Montagu) 1905 – 1999; English American anthropologist & author.

It is in our lives and not our words that our religion must be read.
- Thomas Jefferson 1743 – 1826; One of the founding fathers of U.S., the principal author of the Declaration of Independence, & 3rd president of U.S.

~Family~

~Family~

It is not what you do for your children, but what you have taught them to do for themselves, that will make them successful human beings.
- Ann Landers (Esther Pauline Lederer) 1918 – 2002; American advice columnist.

An ounce of mother is worth a ton of priests.
- Spanish proverb

Perhaps the greatest social service that can be rendered by anybody to the country and to mankind is to bring up a family.
- George Bernard Shaw 1856 – 1950; Irish playwright, co-founder of London School of Economics, critic, journalist, Nobel Prize winner, & Oscar winner.

No man should bring children into the world who is unwilling to persevere to the end in their nature and education.
- Plato 428 BC – 347 BC; Greek philosopher, mathematician, founder of Academy of Athens (the first institute of higher learning), student of Socrates & teacher of Aristotle.

A truly rich man is one whose children run into his arms when his hands are empty.
- Unknown

If you want your children to turn out well, spend twice as much time with them, and half as much money.
- Abigail Van Buren (Pauline Esther Phillips) AKA "Dear Abby" 1918 – 2013; American advice columnist & radio show host.

If you have never been hated by our child, you have never been a parent.
- Bette Davis 1908 – 1989; American actress.

No family has no ugly member. (There is a black sheep in every flock.)
- *Russian Proverb*

A mother who is really a mother is never free.
- *Honore de Balzac 1799 – 1850; French playwright & novelist.*

Honore de Balzac 1799 – 1850; French playwright & novelist. *A literary artist considered one of the greatest French novelist of all time. Helped develop the traditional form of the novel produced a great number of novels and short stories called "La Comedie humaine" or "The Human Comedy" about French life after the fall of Napoleaon.*

It's when it's small that the cucumber gets warped. (Bad habits
acquired during early life last long; Children should learn good habits from a tender age.)
- *Portuguese Proverb*

So live that you wouldn't be ashamed to sell the family parrot to the town gossip.
- *Will Rogers 1879 – 1935; American humorist, social commentator, actor, & writer.*

For shameful deeds are taught by shameful deeds.
- *Sophocles 497 BC – 405 BC; Ancient Greek playwright.*

People who have good relationships at home are more effective in the marketplace
- Zig Ziglar 1926 – 2012; American author & motivational speaker.

Parents wonder why the streams are bitter, when they themselves have poisoned the fountain.
- John Locke 1632 – 1704; English philosopher & physician.

The first half of our lives is ruined by our parents and second half by our children.
- Clarence Darrow 1857 – 1938; American lawyer, leading member of the ACLU, & defense attorney in the Scopes "Monkey" Trial.

We want our children to fit in and to stand out, even though the goals are conflicting.
- Ellen Goodman 1941 - ; American journalist, columnist, & Pulitzer Prize winner.

The thing that impressed me most about America is the way parents obey their children.
- Edward, the Duke of Windsor 1894 – 1972; English King of the United Kingdom.

The fruit of a tree falls to its root. (The apple does not fall far from the tree. Children observe daily and — in their behavior — often follow the example of their parents.)
- Turkish Proverb

I was so ugly when I was born the doctor slapped everybody.
- Jim Bailey 1949 - ; American singer, film, TV/stage actor, & female impersonator.

As a single withered tree, if set aflame, causes a whole forest to burn, so does a rascal son destroy a whole family.
- Chanakya 370BC – 283BC Indian professor, philosopher, & royal advisor.

~Family~

If a country is to be corruption free and become a nation of beautiful minds, I strongly feel there are three key societal members who can make a difference. They are the father, the mother and the teacher.
- Abdul Kalam 1931; Indian scientist, & 11th president of India.

~Forgiveness~

In taking revenge, a man is but even with his enemy; but in passing it over, he is superior.
- Francis Bacon 1561 – 1626; English philosopher, statesman, scientist, orator, & author.

Hatred, which could destroy so much, never failed to destroy the man who hated, and this was an immutable law.
- James A. Baldwin 1924 – 1987; American playwright, novelist, essayist, poet, critic, & civil rights activist.

It is only imperfection that complains of what is imperfect. The more perfect we are, the gentler and quiet we become towards the defects of others.
- Joseph Addison 1672 – 1719; English poet, playwright, essayist, & politician.

We must develop and maintain the capacity to forgive. He who is devoid of the power to forgive is devoid of the power to love. There is some good in the worst of us and some evil in the best of us.
- Dr. Martin Luther King, Jr. (Michael King) 1929 - 1968; American clergyman, minister, civil rights activist. Nobel Peace Prize, Presidential Medal of Freedom, & Congressional Gold Medal recipient.

No snowflake in an avalanche ever feels responsible.
- Voltaire (Francois-Marie Arouet) 1694 – 1778; French writer, historian, philosopher, & poet.

Respect the burden.
- Napoleon Bonaparte 1769 – 1821; French Emperor, military & political leader. (Referring to life.)

The weak can never forgive. Forgiveness is the attribute of the strong.

- Mahatma Gandhi (Mohandas Karamchand Gandhi) 1869 – 1948; Indian leader of Indian nationalism that used non-violent civil disobedience to lead to Indian independence.

It's easier to get forgiveness than permission.

- Grace Hopper 1906 – 1992; American computer scientist.

There's no point in burying a hatchet if you're going to put up a marker on the site.

- Sydney J. Harris 1917 – 1986; American journalist.

To carry a grudge is like being stung to death by one bee.

- William Walton 1902 – 1983; English composer.

To understand all is to forgive all.

- French Proverb

There is no such thing as part freedom.

- Nelson Mandela 1918 - 2013; South African anti-apartheid revolutionary & former President of South Africa, Nobel Peace Prize, Soviet Order of Lenin, and U.S. Presidential Medal of Freedom recipient

Nelson Mandela 1918 - 2013; South African anti-apartheid revolutionary & former President of South Africa. *A lawyer by trade, Mandela joined the African National Congress and became involved with anti-colonial activities. Both the ANC and Mandela were arrested and unsuccessfully tried for treason on a number of occasions. Following Marxist ideas and goals, Mandela initially set out on a non-violence crusade but later found the militant wing of the party leading a campaign of sabotage against the apartheid government. He was subsequently arrested and convicted of trying to overthrow the government and imprisoned for life in 1961. Due to international pressure, the South African government released him in 1990. Within a few years, Mandela entered negotiations with then president F.W. de Klerk to end apartheid and to establish fair elections. The ANC was victorious electing Mandela as South Africa's first black president. He initiated a new constitution, unified political factions, and initiated a Truth & Reconciliation commission to investigate prior human rights abuses to try to heal the great divide of South African society. Combating poverty, expanding healthcare, and land reform were*

part of some of his other agenda. He refused a second term, instead concentrating on combating HIV, poverty, and focusing on charitable works. Looked on as a communist and terrorist by his critics, Mandela has received over 250 honors including the Nobel Peace Prize, U.S. Presidential Medal of Freedom, the Order of Lenin, and thought of as the father of South Africa.

An army of principles can penetrate where an army of soldiers cannot.
- Thomas Paine 1737 – 1809; English-American author, political activist, theorist, & revolutionary.

Liberty means responsibility. That is why most men dread it.
- George Bernard Shaw 1856 – 1950; Irish playwright, co-founder of London School of Economics, critic, journalist, Nobel Prize winner, & Oscar winner.

To be free is to have achieved your life.
- Tennessee Williams (Thomas Lanier Williams III) 1911 – 1983; American Writer, Playwright, 2 time Pulitzer Prize winner, & Poet.

If we are not free, no one will respect us.
- Abdul Kalam 1931; Indian scientist, & 11th president of India.

No freeman shall be debarred the use of arms.
- Thomas Jefferson 1743 – 1826; One of the founding fathers of U.S., the principal author of the Declaration of Independence, & 3rd president of U.S.

We allow our ignorance to prevail upon us and make us think we can survive alone, alone in patches, alone in groups, alone in races, even alone in genders.
- Maya Angelou (Marguerite Ann Johnson) 1928 - ; American author & poet.

Freedom, in the larger and higher sense, every man must gain for himself.
- Dr. Martin Luther King, Jr. (Michael King) 1929 - 1968; American clergyman, minister, civil rights activist. Nobel Peace Prize, Presidential Medal of Freedom, & Congressional Gold Medal recipient.

64

The shepherd drives the wolf from the sheep for which the sheep thanks the shepherd as a liberator, while the wolf denounces him for the same act as the destroyer of liberty. Plainly, the sheep and the wolf are not agreed upon a definition of liberty.

- Abraham Lincoln 1809 – 1865; American politician, 16th President of the U.S. during the American Civil war & instrumental in abolishing slavery.

Abraham Lincoln 1809 – 1865; American politician, 16th President of the U.S. during the American Civil war & instrumental in abolishing slavery. *Consistently ranked by historians and scholars as one of the greatest U.S. presidents, if not the greatest. Lincoln lost the whole south, but swept the North in order to be elected as President in 1860. Taking this as a sign, seven southern states succeeded from the Union. With most of the southern delegates leaving the government, this gave Lincoln's party firm control over everything. With their newfound powers, the Republicans passed many of their pet bills that allotted free land for colleges in every state, enacted new banking laws, gave free land to settlers and railroad companies, and set up the U.S. Department of Agriculture. Neither side wanted to compromise on slavery and Lincoln famously said, "Both parties deprecated war, but one of them would make war rather*

65

~Freedom~

than let the Nation survive, and the other would accept war rather than let it perish, and the war came." Lincoln was a master politician whose only true aim was to reunite the nation through various political and military maneuvers. In 1863, Lincoln helped push through the Thirteenth Amendment to the U.S. Constitution outlawing slavery. Lincoln was assassinated in 1865 by the actor John Wilkes Booth.

By nature all men are equal in liberty, but not in other endowments.

- Thomas Aquinas 1225 – 1274; Italian friar, priest, philosopher & theologian.

If liberty and equality, as is thought by some, are chiefly to be found in democracy, they will be best attained when all persons alike share in government to the utmost.

- Aristotle 384 BC – 322 BC; Greek philosopher, polymath, and one of the fathers of Western philosophy.

".....all God's children, black men and white men. Jews and Gentiles. Protestants and Catholics will be able to join hands and sing in the words of that old Negro spiritual, "Free at last! Free at last! Thank God almighty, we are free at last!"

- Dr. Martin Luther King, Jr. (Michael King) 1929 - 1968; American clergyman, minister, civil rights activist. Nobel Peace Prize, Presidential Medal of Freedom, & Congressional Gold Medal recipient. Speech in August 1963.

He that would make his own liberty secure, must guard even his enemy from oppression; for if he violates this duty, he establishes a precedent that will reach to himself.

- Thomas Paine 1737 – 1809; English-American author, political activist, theorist, & revolutionary.

66

The God, who gave us life, gave us liberty at the same time.

- Thomas Jefferson 1743 – 1826; One of the founding fathers of U.S., the principal author of the Declaration of Independence, & 3rd president of U.S.

It is not a field of a few acres of ground, but a cause, that we are defending, and whether we defeat the enemy in one battle, or by degrees, the consequences will be the same.

- Thomas Paine 1737 – 1809; English-American author, political activist, theorist, & revolutionary.

That we here highly resolve that these dead shall not have died in vain - that this nation, under God, shall have a new birth of freedom - and that government of the people, by the people, for the people, shall not perish from the earth.

- Abraham Lincoln 1809 – 1865; American politician, 16th President of the U.S. during the American Civil war & instrumental in abolishing slavery.

What then is freedom? The power to live as one wishes.

- Marcus Tullius Cicero 106 BC – 43BC; Roman philosopher, politician, lawyer, orator, political theorist, consul, & constitutionalist.

Justice delayed is justice denied.

- William E. Gladstone 1809 – 1898; English politician & 4 time Prime Minister.

Money won't create success, the freedom to make it will.

- Nelson Mandela 1918 - 2013; South African anti-apartheid revolutionary & former President of South Africa, Nobel Peace Prize, Soviet Order of Lenin, and U.S. Presidential Medal of Freedom recipient.

~Freedom~

Power in defense of freedom is greater than power in behalf of tyranny and oppression, because power, real power, comes from our conviction which produces action, uncompromising action.

- Malcolm X (Malcolm Little) 1925 – 1965; American human & civil rights activist.

Malcolm X (Malcolm Little) 1925 – 1965: American human & civil rights activist. *An active civil rights activist that tried to shed the harshest light on atrocities committed by whites on African Americans. While in prison, Little was hostile to all religions, but began to reconsider his stance when he learned about the Nation of Islam. Malcolm joined the Nation of Islam, which taught black supremacy, separation of races, and rejected integration with whites. He adopted "X" as his last name in 1950 and rejected "Little" which he considered a slave name. After performing the Hajj in Mecca in 1964 and seeing people from all races and backgrounds interacting as equals, Malcolm came to the realization that racial problems were solvable. After returning from Hajj, Malcolm became disillusioned with the Nation of Islam and their teachings by disavowing racism. Stating "I did many things as a Black Muslim that I'm sorry for now. I was a zombie then." Shortly after three members of the Nation of Islam assassinated him. Malcolm X is credited with bringing civil rights to*

the forefront and raising the self-esteem of black Americans while trying to reconnect them with their African heritage.

Arms discourage and keep the invader and plunderer in awe, and preserve order in the world as well as property... Horrid mischief would ensue were the law-abiding deprived of the use of them.
- Thomas Paine 1737 – 1809; English-American author, political activist, theorist, & revolutionary.

In giving freedom to the slave, we assure freedom to the free - honorable alike in what we give and what we preserve. We shall nobly save, or meanly lose, the last best hope of earth.
- Abraham Lincoln 1809 – 1865; American politician, 16th President of the U.S. during the American Civil war & instrumental in abolishing slavery.

~Friendship~

The first method for estimating the intelligence of a ruler is to look at the men he has around him.

- Niccolo Machiavelli 1469 – 1527; Italian historian, politician, diplomat, philosopher, & writer.

Niccolo Machiavelli 1469 – 1527: Italian historian, politician, diplomat, philosopher, & writer. *During his time, Machiavelli was a public official in the Florentine Republic, who had responsibilities in diplomatic and military affairs. In modern terms he was a founder of modern political science and ethics. His most famous book "The Prince" was a manual on how to acquire and retain power by any means necessary.*

He who throws away a friend is as bad as he who throws away his life.

- Sophocles 497 BC – 405 BC; Ancient Greek playwright.

Lie down with dogs, wake up with fleas.

(You will become like your company.)
- English Proverb

A friend to all is a friend to none.

- Aristotle 384 BC – 322 BC; Greek philosopher, polymath, & one of the fathers of Western philosophy.

Friendship with one's self is all important, because without it one cannot be friends with anyone else in the world.

- Anna Eleanor Roosevelt 1884 – 1962; Wife of Franklin D. Roosevelt, diplomat, human rights activist, first lady of the U.S. from 1933 to 1945.

I desire so to conduct the affairs of this administration that if at the end... I have lost every other friend on earth, I shall at least have one friend left, and that friend shall be down inside of me.

- Abraham Lincoln 1809 – 1865; American politician, 16th President of the U.S. during the American Civil war & instrumental in abolishing slavery.

The eyes which don't see each other, forget each other.

- Romanian Proverb

Good friendships are fragile things and require as much care as any other fragile and precious thing.

- Randolph S. Bourne 1886 – 1918; American writer.

Don't walk behind me; I may not lead. Don't walk in front of me; I may not follow. Just walk beside me and be my friend.

- Albert Camus 1913-1960; French author, journalist, philosopher, & Nobel Prize winner in literature.

A friend hears the song in my heart and sings it to me when my memory fails.

- Unknown

If you tell your secret to your friend, you will make him your master.

- Spanish Proverb

~Friendship~

The people who matter will recognize who you are.
- Alan Cohen 1954 - ; American businessman.

People will do anything for those who encourage their dreams, justify their failures, allay their fears, confirm their suspicions and help them throw rocks at their enemies.
- Blair Warren; Unknown.

A friend is known in adversity, like gold is known in fire.
- Slovenian Proverb

There are no strangers here; only friends you haven't yet met.
- William Butler Yeats 1865 – 1939; Irish poet, politician, & Nobel Prize in Literature recipient.

Friendship increases in visiting friends, but in visiting them seldom.
- Francis Bacon 1561 – 1626; English philosopher, statesman, scientist, orator, & author.

The crest and crowning of all good, Life's final star, is Brotherhood.
- Edwin Markham 1852 – 1940; American poet.

Whoever understands how to do a kindness when he fares well would be a friend better than any possession.
- Sophocles 497 BC – 405 BC; Ancient Greek playwright.

Friendship marks a life even more deeply than love. Love risks degenerating into obsession, friendship is never anything but sharing.
- Elie Wiesel 1928 - ; Romanian American professor, author, political activist, & Nobel Peace Prize recipient.

Gifts of enemies are no gifts.
- French Proverb

~Friendship~

Wherever we are, it is our friends that make our world.
- Henry Drummond 1851 – 1897; Scottish evangelist, writer, & lecturer.

What is a friend? A single soul dwelling in two bodies.
- Aristotle 384 BC – 322 BC; Greek philosopher, polymath, & one of the fathers of Western philosophy.

There are people, who the more you do for them, the less they will do for themselves.
- Jane Austen 1775 – 1817; English novelist.

I always felt that the great high privilege, relief and comfort of friendship was that one had to explain nothing.
- Katherine Mansfield 1888 – 1923; New Zealand writer.

In need you will recognize your friends.
(A friend is known in need, like gold is known in fire.)
- Norwegian Proverb

~Government-Politics-Power~

Politics is not a game. It is an earnest business.
- Sir Winston Churchill 1874 – 1965; British Prime Minister 1940-1945 & 1951-1955, historian, artist, & Nobel Prize winner in literature.

Of the twenty-two civilizations that have appeared in history, nineteen of them collapsed when they reached the moral state the United States is in now.
- Arnold J. Toynbee 1889 – 1975; English historian, philosopher of history, & historian.

Political ideology can corrupt the mind, and science.
- E. O. (Edward Osborn) Wilson 1929 - ; American biologist, researcher, theorist, naturalist, & author.

Political necessities sometime turn out to be political mistakes.
- George Bernard Shaw 1856 – 1950; Irish playwright, co-founder of London School of Economics, critic, journalist, Nobel Prize winner, & Oscar winner.

The act of policing is, in order to punish less often, to punish more severely.
- Napoleon Bonaparte 1769 – 1821; French Emperor, military & political leader.

No tendency is quite so strong in human nature as the desire to lay down rules of conduct for other people.
- William Howard Taft 1857 – 1930; American politician, 27th President of the U.S., & Chief Justice of the U.S. after his presidency.

A Bill of Rights is what the people are entitled to against every government, and what no just government should refuse, or rest on inference.

- Thomas Jefferson 1743 – 1826; One of the founding fathers of U.S., the principal author of the Declaration of Independence, & 3rd president of U.S.

Thomas Jefferson 1743 – 1826: One of the founding fathers of U.S., the principal author of the Declaration of Independence, & 3rd president of U.S.A polymath, spoke 5 languages, the first U.S. Secretary of State, organizer of the Democratic-Republican Party, and founder of the University of Virginia. *Jefferson is thought of as one of the greatest U.S. Presidents. He was a strong supporter of science, invention, philosophy, and architecture. His greatness is forever tarnished for ownership of hundreds of slaves, although it is claimed that he opposed slavery, he continued to own hundreds of them even fathering a child with one.*

Today's public figures can no longer write their own speeches or books, and there is some evidence that they can't read them either.

- Gore Vidal 1925 – 2012; American writer, critic, & humorist.

Knowledge is power.

- Dutch Proverb

Developing nations want to become developed nations.
- Abdul Kalam 1931 -; Indian scientist & 11th president of India.

The inherent vice of capitalism is the unequal sharing of blessings; the inherent virtue of socialism is the equal sharing of miseries.
- Sir Winston Churchill 1874 – 1965; British Prime Minister 1940-1945 & 1951-1955, historian, artist, & Nobel Prize winner in literature.

It is dangerous to be right in matters on which the established authorities are wrong.
- Voltaire (Francois-Marie Arouet) 1694 – 1778; French writer, historian, philosopher, & poet.

Good people do not need laws to tell them to act responsibly, while bad people will find a way around the laws.
- Plato 428 BC – 347 BC; Greek philosopher, mathematician, founder of Academy of Athens (the first institute of higher learning), student of Socrates & teacher of Aristotle.

Socialism is the same as Communism, only better English.
- George Bernard Shaw 1856 – 1950; Irish playwright, co-founder of London School of Economics, critic, journalist, Nobel Prize winner, & Oscar winner.

Not necessity, not desire - no, the love of power is the demon of men. Let them have everything - health, food, a place to live, entertainment - they are and remain unhappy and low-spirited: for the demon waits and waits and will be satisfied.
- Friedrich Nietzsche 1844 – 1900; German philosopher, philologist, critic, poet, & composer.

~Government-Politics-Power~

The corporate grip on opinion in the United States is one of the wonders of the Western world. No First World country has ever managed to eliminate so entirely from its media all objectivity - much less dissent.

- Gore Vidal 1925 – 2012; American writer, critic, & humorist.

My dream is of a place and a time where America will once again be seen as the last best hope of earth.

- Abraham Lincoln 1809 – 1865; American politician, 16th President of the U.S. during the American Civil war & instrumental in abolishing slavery.

None but an armed nation can dispense with a standing army. To keep ours armed and disciplined is therefore at all times important.

- Thomas Jefferson 1743 – 1826; One of the founding fathers of U.S., the principal author of the Declaration of Independence, & 3rd president of U.S.

Princes and governments are far more dangerous than other elements within society.

- Niccolo Machiavelli 1469 – 1527; Italian historian, politician, diplomat, philosopher, & writer.

Tyranny naturally arises out of democracy.

- Plato 428 BC – 347 BC; Greek philosopher, mathematician, founder of Academy of Athens (the first institute of higher learning), student of Socrates & teacher of Aristotle.

There is nothing wrong with American that cannot be cured by what is right with America.

- William Jefferson Clinton 1946 - ; American politician, former governor of Arkansas, & 42nd President of the U.S.

He who steals a little steals with the same wish as he who steals much, but with less power.
- Plato 428 BC – 347 BC; Greek philosopher, mathematician, founder of Academy of Athens (the first institute of higher learning), student of Socrates & teacher of Aristotle.

Men should be either treated generously or destroyed, because they take revenge for slight injuries - for heavy ones they cannot.
- Niccolo Machiavelli 1469 – 1527; Italian historian, politician, diplomat, philosopher, & writer.

Patriotism is the willingness to kill and be killed for trivial reason.
- Bertrand Russell 1872 – 1970; English philosopher, logician, mathematician, historian, critic, & Nobel Prize in Literature recipient.

Bertrand Russell 1872 – 1970: English philosopher, logician, mathematician, historian, critic, & Nobel Prize in Literature recipient. *One of the founders of analytic philosophy that emphasis's clarity & argument by logic and precise language, which has become the dominant style of philosophy in the English speaking world. He's had increasing influence on logic, mathematics, language, AI, computer science, philosophy, epistemology, & metaphysics.*

In politics, as in religion, it is equally absurd to aim at making proselytes by fire and sword. Heresies in either can rarely be cured by persecution.

- Alexander Hamilton 1757 – 1804; American colonial politician, one of the founding fathers of the U.S., Secretary of the treasury, & statesmen.

In great contests each party claims to act in accordance with the will of God. Both may be, and one must be wrong.

- Abraham Lincoln 1809 – 1865; American politician, 16th President of the U.S. during the American Civil war & instrumental in abolishing slavery.

Democracy... while it lasts is bloodier than either aristocracy or monarchy. Remember, democracy never lasts long. It soon wastes, exhausts, and murders itself. There is never a democracy that did not commit suicide.

- John Adams 1735 – 1826; American Politician, 2nd President of the U.S., a founding father of the U.S., diplomat, & first Vice President of the U.S.

Politics is such a torment that I advise everyone I love not to mix with it.

- Thomas Jefferson 1743 – 1826; One of the founding fathers of U.S., the principal author of the Declaration of Independence, & 3rd president of U.S.

All national institutions of churches, whether Jewish, Christian or Turkish, appear to me no other than human inventions, set up to terrify and enslave mankind, and monopolize power and profit.

- Thomas Paine 1737 – 1809; English-American author, political activist, theorist, & revolutionary.

Peace, commerce and honest friendship with all nations; entangling alliances with none.

- Thomas Jefferson 1743 – 1826; One of the founding fathers of U.S., the principal author of the Declaration of Independence, & 3rd president of U.S.

You can always count on Americans to do the right thing - after they've tried everything else.

- Sir Winston Churchill 1874 – 1965; British Prime Minister 1940-1945 & 1951-1955, historian, artist, & Nobel Prize winner in literature.

Political tags - such as royalist, communist, democrat, populist, fascist, liberal, conservative, and so forth - are never basic criteria. The human race divides politically into those who want people to be controlled and those who have no such desire.

- Robert A. Heinlein 1907 – 1988; American award winning science fiction writer.

Democracy is supposed to give you the feeling of choice, like Painkiller X and Painkiller Y. But they're both just aspirin.

- Gore Vidal 1925 – 2012; American writer, critic, & humorist.

When you look at the long history of man, you see that more hideous crimes have been committed in the name of obedience than have been committed in the name of rebellion.

- C. P. (Charles Percy) Snow 1905 – 1980; English chemist & novelist.

No Justice, no peace!

- Al Sharpton 1954 - ; American minister, civil rights activist, & TV/radio talk show host.

80

~Government-Politics-Power~

The higher you climb, the greater you fall. (Slip-ups becomes more consequential, the more influence you have.)
- *Vietnamese Proverb*

Labor is prior to, and independent of, capital. Capital is only the fruit of labor, and could never have existed if labor had not first existed. Labor is the superior of capital, and deserves much the higher consideration.
- *Abraham Lincoln 1809 – 1865; American politician, 16th President of the U.S. during the American Civil war & instrumental in abolishing slavery.*

The more laws and order are made prominent, the more thieves and robbers there will be.
- *Lao Tzu (Laozi) 6th century BC; Ancient Chinese philosopher.*

I believe that banking institutions are more dangerous to our liberties than standing armies.
- *Thomas Jefferson 1743 – 1826; One of the founding fathers of U.S., the principal author of the Declaration of Independence, & 3rd president of U.S.*

It is not the function of government to keep the citizen from falling into error; it is the function of the citizen to keep the government from falling into error.
- *Robert H. Jackson 1892 – 1954; American Lawyer, U.S. Attorney General, & Associate Justice of the U.S. Supreme Court.*

The worst thing in this world, next to anarchy, is government.
- *Henry Ward Beecher 1813-1887; American clergymen, speaker, & abolitionist.*

Let the welfare of the people be the supreme law.
- *Latin Proverb*

Do you know what astonished me most in the world? The inability of force to create anything. In the long run, the sword is always beaten by the spirit.

- Napoleon Bonaparte 1769 – 1821; French Emperor, military & political leader. Stated near the end of his life.

Napoleon Bonaparte 1769 – 1821: French Emperor, military & political leader. *In part to the victories in Napoleonic wars, Napoleon is considered as one of the greatest military commanders. His strategy and tactics are still studied at military academies around the world.*

Make crime pay. Become a lawyer.

- Will Rogers 1879 – 1935; American humorist, social commentator, actor, & writer.

Capitalism has destroyed our belief in any effective power but that of self-interest backed by force.

- George Bernard Shaw 1856 – 1950; Irish playwright, co-founder of London School of Economics, critic, journalist, Nobel Prize winner, & Oscar winner.

Democracy arises out of the notion that those who are equal in any respect are equal in all respects; because men are equally free, they claim to be absolutely equal.

- Aristotle 384 BC – 322 BC; Greek philosopher, polymath, & one of the fathers of Western philosophy.

The spirit of this country is totally adverse to a large military force.

- Thomas Jefferson 1743 – 1826; One of the founding fathers of U.S., the principal author of the Declaration of Independence, & 3rd president of U.S.

Poverty is the worst form of violence.

- Mahatma Gandhi (Mohandas Karamchand Gandhi) 1869 – 1948; Indian leader of Indian nationalism that used non-violent civil disobedience to lead to Indian independence.

This and no other is the root from which a tyrant springs; when he first appears he is a protector.

- Plato 428 BC – 347 BC; Greek philosopher, mathematician, founder of Academy of Athens (the first institute of higher learning), student of Socrates & teacher of Aristotle.

Authority, not truth, makes law.

- Latin Proverb

Human society could not exist one hour except on the basis of law which holds the baser passions of men in restraint.

- Kelly Miller 1863 – 1939; American mathematician, sociologist, essayist, professor, & civil rights activist.

Illegal aliens have always been a problem in the United States. Ask any Indian.

- Robert Orben 1927 - ; American comedy writer, author, & speech writer to the President Gerald Ford.

The rich will do anything for the poor but get off their backs.
- *Karl Marx 1818 – 1883; German philosopher, economist, sociologist, historian, journalist, & author.*

Karl Marx 1818 – 1883: German philosopher, economist, sociologist, historian, journalist, & author. *As an economist he developed his ideas on labor's relation to capital, which continues to influence economic thought. His most famous books on the subject were "The Communist Manifesto" and "Das Kapital". Marx's ideas are known as Marxism, which holds that societies are always in conflict between the working class and ownership class. Marx believed that the wealthy ownership class prefers capitalism because it benefits them the most over the working class, which would inevitably lead to its own self destruction ending in a dictatorship and ultimately in a classless society like communism. Marx actively lobbied for communism and for the people to bring about socio-economic changes. His ideas took power in many countries like the former Soviet Union, China, and Cuba.*

We have the best government that money can buy.
- *Mark Twain (Samuel Langhorne Clemens) 1835-1910; American author & humorist.*

There are two kinds of criminals, those who get caught and the rest of us.
- *Unknown*

When a man assumes a public trust he should consider himself a public property.
- Thomas Jefferson 1743 – 1826; One of the founding fathers of U.S., the principal author of the Declaration of Independence, & 3rd president of U.S.

Human progress is neither automatic nor inevitable... Every step toward the goal of justice requires sacrifice, suffering, and struggle; the tireless exertions and passionate concern of dedicated individuals.
- Dr. Martin Luther King, Jr. (Michael King) 1929 - 1968; American clergyman, minister, civil rights activist. Nobel Peace Prize, Presidential Medal of Freedom, & Congressional Gold Medal recipient.

Our success as a nation is not measured by how many years we have governed or how many wars we have won. It is measured by the quality of life which we have created for the society that our ideals were founded upon.
- Matthew Morgan 1988 - ; Writer.

A criminal is a person with predatory instincts who lacks the capital to form a corporation.
- Howard Scott 1890 – 1970; American engineer.

A man's respect for law and order exists in precise relationship to the size of his paycheck.
- Adam Clayton Powell Jr. 1908 – 1972; American politician, & pastor.

Why, in our age of science, do we still have laws and policies which come from an age of superstition?
- Shereen El Feki; Arab writer.

Americans are like a rich father who wishes he knew how to give his son the hardships that made him rich.
- Robert Lee Frost 1874-1963; American Poet, Congressional Gold Medal winner.

Even when laws have been written down, they ought not always to remain unaltered.
- Aristotle 384 BC – 322 BC; Greek philosopher, polymath, & one of the fathers of Western philosophy.

I was in prison before entering here....The solitude, the long moments of meditative contemplation, have given me the key to my freedom.
- Malcolm X (Malcolm Little) 1925 – 1965; American human & civil rights activist.

I have sworn upon the altar of God, eternal hostility against every form of tyranny over the mind of man.
- Thomas Jefferson 1743 – 1826; One of the founding fathers of U.S., the principal author of the Declaration of Independence, & 3rd president of U.S.

Injustice anywhere is a threat to justice everywhere.
- Dr. Martin Luther King, Jr. (Michael King) 1929 - 1968; American clergyman, minister, civil rights activist. Nobel Peace Prize, Presidential Medal of Freedom, & Congressional Gold Medal recipient.

The only way to make sure people you agree with can speak is to support the rights of people you don't agree with.
- Eleanor Holmes Norton 1937 – American politician.

A fool and his money are soon elected.
- Will Rogers 1879 – 1935; American humorist, social commentator, actor, & writer.

Power is the ability not to have to please.
- Elizabeth Janeway 1913 – 2005; American author & critic.

If there is no struggle, there is no progress….Power concedes nothing without a demand.

- Frederick Douglas (Fredrick Augustus Washington Bailey) 1818 – 1895; American orator, writer, statesman, abolitionist, former slave, & autobiographer.

Frederick Douglas (Fredrick Augustus Washington Bailey) 1818 – 1895: American orator, writer, statesman, abolitionist, former slave, & autobiographer. *Douglas was a former runaway slave that became the leader of abolitionist movement. Douglas was a gifted orator and writer that shook the white establishment's idea that African Americans didn't have the intellectual ability to be independent citizens. Many couldn't believe that a slave could have such great oratory skills. Douglas worked tirelessly after the war for equality for all people.*

A lawyer with a briefcase can steal more than a thousand men with guns.

- Mario Puzo 1920 – 1999; Italian American author, novelist, & screenwriter.

When reform becomes impossible, revolution becomes imperative.

- Kelly Miller 1863 – 1939; American mathematician, sociologist, essayist, professor, & civil rights activist.

In the act of resistance, the rudiments of freedom are already present.
- Angela Davis 1944 - ; American political activist, professor, scholar, & author.

Every prisoner is not a criminal, just as every criminal is not in prison.
- Michael Eric Dyson 1958 - ; American author, professor, & radio talk show host.

In order to be the master, the politician poses as the servant.
- Charles De Gaulle 1890 – 1970; French general & president of the French Fifth Republic.

Republicans stand for raw, unbridled evil and greed and ignorance smothered in balloons and ribbons.
- Frank Zappa 1940 – 1993; American musician, songwriter, composer, producer, & director.

A bureaucrat is a Democrat who holds an office that a Republican wants.
- Harry S. Truman 1884 – 1972; American politician & 33rd President of the United States.

If your opponent is drowning, throw him an anvil.
- James Carville 1944 - ; American political strategist, commentator, & media personality.

I'm all for foreign aid, and the sooner we get it the better.
- Bob Hope 1903 – 2003; English American comedian, actor, singer, dancer, author, vaudevillian.

Unfortunately the prisons often reproduce the pathology that they seek to eliminate.
- Michael Eric Dyson 1958 - ; American author, professor, & radio talk show host.

Against the assault of laughter nothing can stand.
- Mark Twain (Samuel Langhorne Clemens) 1835-1910; American author & humorist.

In parts of America today, it's more acceptable to carry a handgun than a pack of cigarettes.
- Katharine Whitehorn 1928 - ; English journalist, writer, & columnist.

Republics decline into democracies and democracies degenerate into despotisms.
- Aristotle 384 BC – 322 BC; Greek philosopher, polymath, & one of the fathers of Western philosophy.

Property is surely a right of mankind as real as liberty.
John Adams 1735 – 1826; 2nd President of the U.S., a founding father of the U.S., diplomat, & first Vice President of the U.S.

The Constitution shall never be construed… to prevent the people of the United States who are peaceable citizens from keeping their own arms.
- Samuel Adams 1722 – 1803; American politician, statesman, political philosopher, & one of the founding father of the U.S.

Liberalism is trust of the people tempered by prudence. Conservatism is distrust of the people tempered by fear.
- William E. Gladstone 1809 – 1898; English politician & 4 time Prime Minister.

The cornerstone of all great modern civilizations will continue to be freedom, justice, & equality. One cannot stand without the others.
- M.I. Seka 1972 - ; Author & businessman.

We are often deterred from crime by the disgrace of others.
- Horace 65 BC – 8 BC; Roman poet.

~Happiness & Contentment~

Rule #1 of life. Do what makes YOU happy.
- Unknown

Human felicity (high degree of happiness) is produced not as much by great pieces of good fortune that seldom happen as by little advantages that occur every day.
- Benjamin Franklin 1706 – 1790; American politician, One of the founding fathers of the U.S., polymath, author, postmaster, scientist, musician, inventor, statesmen, critic, & diplomat.

If thou wilt make a man happy, add not unto his riches but take away from his desires.
- Epicurus 341 BC – 270 BC; Greek philosopher.

Happiness is not being pained in body or troubled in mind.
- Thomas Jefferson 1743 – 1826; One of the founding fathers of U.S., the principal author of the Declaration of Independence, & 3rd president of U.S.

Happiness is not an ideal of reason, but of imagination.
- Immanuel Kant 1724 – 1804; German philosopher.

When a man has lost all happiness, he's not alive. Call him a breathing corpse.
- Sophocles 497 BC – 405 BC; Ancient Greek playwright.

There is no austerity equal to a balanced mind, and there is no happiness equal to contentment; there is no disease like covetousness, and no virtue like mercy.
- Chanakya 370BC – 283BC Indian professor, philosopher, & royal advisor.

The art of being happy lies in the power of extracting happiness from common things.
- Henry Ward Beecher 1813-1887; American clergymen, speaker, & abolitionist.

If we become uncomfortable in any given moment, we can look at a flower, a pebble in the street or the tire on our car and be grateful. We can gaze at a person in the distance or at a cloud in the sky and be appreciative. We can smile at a stranger, hug someone we know or tidy a disorganized shelf and be thankful for the opportunity. If we choose gratitude, we will be happy!
- Barry Neil Kaufman; Unknown.

A man should always consider how much he has more than he wants.
- Joseph Addison 1672 – 1719; English poet, playwright, essayist, & politician.

You never achieve success unless you like what you are doing.
- Dale Carnegie 1888 – 1955; American writer, lecturer, & self-improvement coach.

Very little is needed to make a happy life; it is all within yourself, in your way of thinking.
- Marcus Aurelius 121 AD – 180 AD; Roman Emperor, & philosopher.

~Happiness & Contentment~

Happiness is neither virtue nor pleasure nor this thing nor that but simply growth, we are happy when we are growing.
- William Butler Yeats 1865 – 1939; Irish poet, politician, & Nobel Prize in Literature recipient.

The person who seeks all their applause from outside has their happiness in another's keeping.
- Dale Carnegie 1888 – 1955; American writer, lecturer, & self-improvement coach.

If you're not feeling good about you, what you're wearing outside doesn't mean a thing.
- Leontyne Price 1927 - ; American opera singer.

The talent for being happy is appreciating and liking what you have, instead of what you don't have.
- Woody Allen (Allan Stewart Konigsberg) 1935 - ; American comedian, screenwriter, director, actor, author, playwright, musician, & Academy Award winner.

The discontented man finds no easy chair.
- Benjamin Franklin 1706 – 1790; American politician, One of the founding fathers of the U.S., polymath, author, postmaster, scientist, musician, inventor, statesmen, critic, & diplomat.

Let not your mind run on what you lack as much as on what you have already.
- Marcus Aurelius 121 AD – 180 AD; Roman Emperor, & philosopher.

Happiness is an inside job.
- William Arthur Ward 1921 – 1994; American author.

The best way to cheer yourself up is to try to cheer somebody else up.
- Mark Twain (Samuel Langhorne Clemens) 1835-1910; American author & humorist.

~Happiness & Contentment~

Even a happy life cannot be without a measure of darkness, and the word happy would lose its meaning if it were not balanced by sadness. It is far better to take things as they come along with patience and equanimity.
- C. G. (Carl Gustav) Jung 1875 – 1961; Swiss psychiatrist & psychotherapist.

Happiness is not a goal; it is a by-product.
- Anna Eleanor Roosevelt 1884 – 1962; Wife of Franklin D. Roosevelt, diplomat, human rights activist, first lady of the U.S. from 1933 to 1945.

The walls we build around us to keep sadness out also keeps out the joy.
- Jim Rohn 1930 – 2009; American entrepreneur, author, & motivational speaker.

Happiness does not lie in happiness, but in the achievement of it.
- Fyodor Mikhailovis Dostoyevsky 1821 – 1881; Russian novelist, philosopher, & writer.

Contentment consist not in adding more fuel, but in taking away some fire.
- Thomas Fuller 1608 – 1661; English historian & writer.

When you are content to be simply yourself and don't compare or compete, everybody will respect you.
- Lao Tzu (Laozi) 6th century BC; Ancient Chinese philosopher.

~Health & Beauty~

Let the beauty that we love be what we do.
- Rumi (Jalal Ad-Din Muhammad Balkhi/Rumi) 1207 – 1273; Persian (present day Tajikistan) poet, theologian, Sufi mystic, & jurist.

Rumi (Jalal Ad-Din Muhammad Balkhi/Rumi) 1207 – 1273: Persian (present day Tajikistan) poet, theologian, Sufi mystic, & jurist. *Considered to be one of the greatest poets that ever lived. Rumi's general poetic theme is one of mans separation from his roots and his great desire to become one with it. He advocated mystical journey for the truth, love, ego abandonment, and enlightenment. The journey ends with the traveler returning with higher maturity, love, and a sense of service to all of creation without discrimination to beliefs, race, class, or nation.*

Music is a moral law. It gives soul to the universe, wings to the mind, flight to the imagination, and charm and gaiety to life and to everything.
- Plato 428 BC – 347 BC; Greek philosopher, mathematician, founder of Academy of Athens (the first institute of higher learning), student of Socrates & teacher of Aristotle.

Whoever neglects the arts when he is young has lost the past and is dead to the future.
- Sophocles 497 BC – 405 BC; Ancient Greek playwright.

A picture is a poem without words.
- Horace 65 BC – 8 BC; Roman poet.

Art enables us to find ourselves and lose ourselves at the same time.
- Thomas Merton 1915 – 1968; French American writer & mystic.

No great artist ever sees things as they really are. If he did, he would cease to be an artist.
- Oscar Wilde 1854 – 1900; Irish writer, poet, & playwright.

Take care of your body. It's the only place you have to live.
- Jim Rohn 1930 – 2009; American entrepreneur, author, & motivational speaker.

Style is knowing who you are, what you want to say, and not giving a damn.
- Gore Vidal 1925 – 2012; American writer, critic, & humorist.

If you can't see anything beautiful about yourself, get a better mirror.
- Shane Koyczan 1976 - ; Canadian poet & writer.

When I told my doctor I couldn't afford an operation, he offered to touch-up my X-rays.
- Henny Youngman 1906 – 1998; English American comedian.

The secret of health for both mind and body is not to mourn for the past, worry about the future, or anticipate troubles, but to live in the present moment wisely and earnestly.
- Buddha 563 BCE – 483 BCE; Sage that taught principles that Buddhism was founded on.

Everybody needs beauty as well as bread, places to play in and pray in, where nature may heal and give strength to body and soul.
- John Muir 1838 – 1914; Scottish American naturalist, author, & conservationist.

Art is the most intense mode of individualism that the world has known.
- Oscar Wilde 1854 – 1900; Irish writer, poet, & playwright.

An artist is not paid for his labor but for his vision.
- James Whistler 1834 – 1903; American English artist.

The artist is nothing without the gift, but the gift is nothing without work.
- Emile Zola 1840 – 1902; French writer.

The obvious is that which is never seen until someone expresses it simply.
- Khalil Gibran 1883 – 1931; Lebanese artist, poet, & writer.

No great man lives in vain. The history of the world is but the biography of great men.
- Thomas Carlyle 1795 – 1881; Scottish philosopher, writer, historian, essayist, satirist, & teacher.

Of the twenty-two civilizations that have appeared in history, nineteen of them collapsed when they reached the moral state the United States is in now.
- Arnold J. Toynbee 1889 – 1975; English historian, philosopher of history, & historian.

Indeed, history is nothing more than a tableau of crimes and misfortunes.
- Voltaire (Francois-Marie Arouet) 1694 – 1778; French writer, historian, philosopher, & poet.

Men make history and not the other way around. In periods where there is no leadership, society stands still. Progress occurs when courageous, skillful leaders seize the opportunity to change things for the better.
- Harry S. Truman 1884 – 1972; American politician & 33rd President of the United States.

History does not long entrust the care of freedom to the weak or the timid.
- Dwight D. Eisenhower 1890 – 1969; American politician, 34th President of the U.S., 5 star general, Supreme Commander of Allied forces in Europe & Supreme Commander of NATO.

So many people of color who made major contributions to American history have been trapped in the purgatory of history.
- Henry Louis Gates, Jr. 1950 - ; American literary critic, educator, scholar, writer, & editor.

White people sending black people to make war on yellow people in order to defend the land they stole from the red people.
- Stokely Carmichael 1941 – 1998; Trinidadian American civil rights activist. Describing the Vietnam War.

There is no king who has not had a slave among his ancestors, and no slave who has not had a king among his.

- Helen Adams Keller 1880 – 1968; American author, political activist, first deaf-blind person to earn a B.A. & lecturer.

Helen Adams Keller 1880 – 1968: American author, political activist, first deaf blind person to earn a B.A. & lecturer. *As a baby Keller contracted an illness that left her deaf and blind. Ann Sullivan was a former student of Perkins institute for the Blind, visually impaired herself, set out to assist Keller with communicating with the outside world. Through many frustrated sessions, Sullivan's breakthrough came when Keller realized that each object had a unique name describing it when one day Sullivan was teaching Keller the word "water" while running her hand under water. This breakthrough shattered Keller's world and set her into a lifetime of exploration and advocacy. Keller would go on to become a prolific author, a champion of women's suffrage, labor rights, and one of the founders of the ACLU. Her birthday is federally commemorated on June 27 in the U.S.*

98

Revolutions are the locomotives of history.
- Karl Marx 1818 – 1883; German philosopher, economist, sociologist, historian, journalist, & author.

The past actually happened but history is only what someone wrote down.
- A. Whitney Brown 1952 - ; American comedian & Emmy Award Winner.

Judging from the main portions of the history of the world, so far, justice is always in jeopardy.
- Walt Whitman 1819 – 1892; American essayist, journalist, humanist & poet.

History is always changing.
- Aung San Suu Kyi 1945 - ; Burmese politician. Nobel Peace Prize, Congressional Gold Medal, & Presidential Medal of Freedom recipient.

History never looks like history when you are living through it.
- John W. Gardner 1912 – 2002; American author, Secretary of Health, Education, & Welfare, & Presidential Medal of Freedom recipient.

History is a vast early warning system.
- Norman Cousins 1915 – 1990; American political journalist, author, professor, & world Peace Advocate.

History is a tool used by politicians to justify their intentions.
- Ted Koppel (Edward James Martin Koppel) 1940 - ; English American broadcast journalist.

You have to look at history as an evolution of society.
- Jean Chretien 1934 - ; Canadian politician & 20th Prime Minister of Canada.

Study history, study history. In history lie all the secrets of statecraft.
- Sir Winston Churchill 1874 – 1965; British Prime Minister 1940-1945 & 1951-1955, historian, artist, & Nobel Prize winner in literature.

That great dust-heap called 'history'.
- Augustine Birrell 1850 – 1933; English politician, barrister, academic & author.

Blood alone moves the wheels of history.
- Martin Luther 1483 – 1546; German monk, Catholic priest, & professor of theology.

The course of history can be changed but not halted.
- Paul Robeson 1898 – 1976; American singer, actor, & civil rights activist.

Skepticism is a virtue in history as well as in philosophy.
- Napoleon Bonaparte 1769 – 1821; French Emperor, military & political leader.

~Justice & Equality~

Genocide is the logical conclusion of racism.
- James Cone 1938 - ; American theologian.

It is better to risk saving a guilty man than to condemn an innocent one.
- Voltaire (Francois-Marie Arouet) 1694 – 1778; French writer, historian, philosopher, & poet.

I believe in the equality of man; and I believe that religious duties consist in doing justice, loving mercy, and endeavoring to make our fellow-creatures happy.
- Thomas Paine 1737 – 1809; English-American author, political activist, theorist, & revolutionary.

Whoever fights monsters should see to it that in the process he does not become a monster. And if you gaze long enough into an abyss, the abyss will gaze back into you.
- Friedrich Nietzsche 1844 – 1900; German philosopher, philologist, critic, poet, & composer.

Important principles may, and must, be inflexible.
- Abraham Lincoln 1809 – 1865; American politician, 16th President of the U.S. during the American Civil war & instrumental in abolishing slavery.

Once the game is over, the king and the pawn go back in the same box.
- Italian Proverb

A good and faithful judge ever prefers the honorable to the expedient.
- Horace 65 BC – 8 BC; Roman poet.

I think the first duty of society is justice.

- Alexander Hamilton 1757 – 1804; American colonial politician, one of the founding fathers of the U.S., Secretary of the treasury, & statesmen.

Alexander Hamilton 1757 – 1804: American colonial politician, one of the founding fathers of the U.S., Secretary of the treasury, & statesmen. *Hamilton was a prominent figure in early American history. Was the chief author of economic policies of Washington, believed in a strong central government, wanted to create a government owned central bank, and assume state debts by levying tariffs on imports and excise tax. Hamilton died after being mortally wounded in a duel with Aaron Burr.*

All men are by nature equal, made all of the same earth by one Workman; and however we deceive ourselves, as dear unto God is the poor peasant as the mighty prince.

- Plato 428 BC – 347 BC; Greek philosopher, mathematician, founder of Academy of Athens (the first institute of higher learning), student of Socrates & teacher of Aristotle.

Poverty is the mother of crime.

- Marcus Aurelius 121 AD – 180 AD; Roman Emperor, & philosopher.

It is error only, and not truth, that shrinks from inquiry.
- Thomas Paine 1737 – 1809; English-American author, political activist, theorist, & revolutionary.

Insanity in individuals is something rare - but in groups, parties, nations and epochs, it is the rule.
- Friedrich Nietzsche 1844 – 1900; German philosopher, philologist, critic, poet, & composer.

The ignorant are always prejudiced and the prejudiced are always ignorant.
- Charles V. 1500 – 1558; Holy Roman Empire Emperor.

The opposite of poverty is not wealth. ... In too many places, the opposite of poverty is justice.
- Bryan Stevenson 1959 –; American professor & founder of the Equal Justice Initiative.

Injustice in the end produces independence.
- Voltaire (Francois-Marie Arouet) 1694 – 1778; French writer, historian, philosopher, & poet.

This fact of nature (skin color) offers no clue to the character of quality of the person underneath.
- Marian Anderson 1897 – 1993; American singer & civil rights activist.

These men ask for just the same thing, fairness, and fairness only. This, so far as in my power, they, and all others, shall have.
- Abraham Lincoln 1809 – 1865; American politician, 16th President of the U.S. during the American Civil war & instrumental in abolishing slavery.

~Justice & Equality~

It is right to give every man his due.

- Plato 428 BC – 347 BC; Greek philosopher, mathematician, founder of Academy of Athens (the first institute of higher learning), student of Socrates & teacher of Aristotle.

Plato 428 BC – 347 BC: Greek philosopher, mathematician, founder of Academy of Athens (the first institute of higher learning), student of Socrates & teacher of Aristotle. *Plato was an important figure in laying of the foundation of Western philosophy; his writings have been used to teach philosophy, logic, ethics, religion, and mathematics.*

The genius of our ruling class is that it has kept a majority of the people from ever questioning the inequity of a system where most people drudge along, paying heavy taxes for which they get nothing in return.

- Gore Vidal 1925 – 2012; American writer, critic, & humorist.

I believe in the equality of man; and I believe that religious duties consist in doing justice, loving mercy, and endeavoring to make our fellow-creatures happy.

- Thomas Paine 1737 – 1809; English-American author, political activist, theorist, & revolutionary.

Equality is the heart and essence of democracy, freedom, and justice.

- Asa Philip Randolph 1869 – 1979; American civil rights leader & labor leader.

Fidelity (Loyalty, keeping a promise) is the sister of justice.

- Horace 65 BC – 8 BC; Roman poet.

The spirit of resistance to government is so valuable on certain occasions that I wish it to be always kept alive.

- Thomas Jefferson 1743 – 1826; One of the founding fathers of U.S., the principal author of the Declaration of Independence, & 3rd president of U.S.

A soul that is kind and intends justice discovers more than any sophist (philosopher).

- Sophocles 497 BC – 405 BC; Ancient Greek playwright.

I know one race, the human race.

- Osceola M. Adams 1890 – 1983; American actress, teacher, director, & clothing designer.

Let's have faith that right makes might; and in that faith let us, to the end, dare to do our duty as we understand it.

- Abraham Lincoln 1809 – 1865; American politician, 16th President of the U.S. during the American Civil war & instrumental in abolishing slavery.

The highest reach of injustice is to be deemed just when you are not.

-Plato 428 BC – 347 BC; Greek philosopher, mathematician, founder of Academy of Athens (the first institute of higher learning), student of Socrates & teacher of Aristotle.

Time alone reveals the just man; but you might discern a bad man in a single day.
- Sophocles 497 BC – 405 BC; Ancient Greek playwright.

The probability that we may fail in the struggle ought not to deter us from the support of a cause we believe to be just.
- Abraham Lincoln 1809 – 1865; American politician, 16th President of the U.S. during the American Civil war & instrumental in abolishing slavery.

~Justice & Equality~

~Knowledge & Education~

One of the joys of reading is the ability to plug into the shared wisdom of mankind.

- Ishmael Reed 1938 - ; American poet, essayist, songwriter, playwright, & novelist.

The doors of wisdom are never shut.

- Benjamin Franklin 1706 – 1790; American politician, One of the founding fathers of the U.S., polymath, author, postmaster, scientist, musician, inventor, statesmen, critic, & diplomat.

In youth we learn, in age we understand.

- Marie Ebner-Eschenbach 1830 – 1916; Austrian writer.

Simulated disorder postulates perfect discipline; simulated fear postulates courage; simulated weakness postulates strength.

- Lao Tzu (Laozi) 6th century BC; Ancient Chinese philosopher.

Knowledge without education is but armed injustice.

- Horace 65 BC – 8 BC; Roman poet.

What we want is to see the child in pursuit of knowledge, and not knowledge in pursuit of the child.

- George Bernard Shaw 1856 – 1950; Irish playwright, co-founder of London School of Economics, critic, journalist, Nobel Prize winner, & Oscar winner.

Those who educate children well are more to be honored than they who produce them; for one only gave them life, those the art of living well.

- Aristotle 384 BC – 322 BC; Greek philosopher, polymath, & one of the fathers of Western philosophy.

The doer alone learneth.

- Friedrich Nietzsche 1844 – 1900; German philosopher, philologist, critic, poet, & composer.

Friedrich Nietzsche 1844 – 1900; German philosopher, philologist, critic, poet, & composer.
Central to his philosophy was the idea of "life-affirmation" which involved the questioning of any and all doctrines, regardless of how entrenched those views were in culture (such as religion). He wanted to reveal the motives widely held behind those ideas and get to what he believed were the core truths. Raised in a religious household, he lost faith at the age of 20 and wrote a famous letter to his deeply religious sister, saying: "Hence the ways of men part: if you wish to strive for peace of soul and pleasure, then believe; if you wish to be a devotee of truth, then inquire..." He died of a stroke at the rather young age of 55.

To make headway, improve your head.

- B. C. Forbes 1880 – 1954; Scottish-American financial journalist, author, & founder of Forbes Magazine.

You can rule ignorance; you can manipulate the illiterate; you can do whatever you want when a people are uneducated, so that goes in line with corrupt business and corrupt politics.

- Will.I.Am (William James Adams) 1975 - ; American recording artist, songwriter, & producer.

~Knowledge & Education~

Don't just read the easy stuff. You may be entertained by it, but you will never grow from it.
- Jim Rohn 1930 – 2009; American entrepreneur, author, & motivational speaker.

It is terrible to speak well and be wrong.
- Sophocles 497 BC – 405 BC; Ancient Greek playwright.

It is your prime responsibility to acquire useful knowledge from others and to apply it appropriately. You don't have to reinvent the wheel, but you do have to learn from those who did.
- Gary Ryan Blair; American Businessman.

The direction in which education starts a man will determine his future in life.
- Plato 428 BC – 347 BC; Greek philosopher, mathematician, founder of Academy of Athens (the first institute of higher learning), student of Socrates & teacher of Aristotle.

The power to question is the basis of all human progress.
- Mahatma Gandhi (Mohandas Karamchand Gandhi) 1869 – 1948; Indian leader of Indian nationalism that used non-violent civil disobedience to lead to Indian independence.

Genius without education is like silver in the mine.
- Benjamin Franklin 1706 – 1790; American politician, One of the founding fathers of the U.S., polymath, author, postmaster, scientist, musician, inventor, statesmen, critic, & diplomat.

All men are born with a nose and ten fingers, but no one was born with a knowledge of God.
- Voltaire (Francois-Marie Arouet) 1694 – 1778; French writer, historian, philosopher, & poet.

Live for a century — learn for a century.
– Russian Proverb

Our treasure lies in the beehive of our knowledge. We are perpetually on the way thither, being by nature winged insects and honey gatherers of the mind.
- Friedrich Nietzsche 1844 – 1900; German philosopher, philologist, critic, poet, & composer.

I do not think much of a man who is not wiser today than he was yesterday.
- Abraham Lincoln 1809 – 1865; American politician, 16th President of the U.S. during the American Civil war & instrumental in abolishing slavery.

Opinion is the medium between knowledge and ignorance.
- Plato 428 BC – 347 BC; Greek philosopher, mathematician, founder of Academy of Athens (the first institute of higher learning), student of Socrates & teacher of Aristotle.

A wise man can learn more from a foolish question than a fool can learn from a wise answer.
- Bruce Lee 1940 - 1973; American martial artist, actor, filmmaker, & pop culture icon.

The trouble with the world is that the stupid are cocksure and the intelligent are full of doubt.
- Bertrand Russell 1872 – 1970; English philosopher, logician, mathematician, historian, critic, & Nobel Prize in Literature recipient.

To penetrate and dissipate these clouds of darkness, the general mind must be strengthened by education.
- Thomas Jefferson 1743 – 1826; One of the founding fathers of U.S., the principal author of the Declaration of Independence, & 3rd president of U.S.

Integrity without knowledge is weak and useless, and knowledge without integrity is dangerous and dreadful.
Samuel Johnson 1709 – 1784; English writer, poet, essayist, critic, editor, & author of the first English dictionary.

~Knowledge & Education~

Knowledge is the food of the soul.

- Plato 428 BC – 347 BC; Greek philosopher, mathematician, founder of Academy of Athens (the first institute of higher learning), student of Socrates & teacher of Aristotle.

We cannot teach people anything; we can only help them discover it within themselves.

- Galileo Galilei 1564 – 1642; Italian physicist, mathematician, astronomer, & philosopher & polymath.

He who would learn to fly one day must first learn to stand and walk and run and climb and dance; one cannot fly into flying.

- Friedrich Nietzsche 1844 – 1900; German philosopher, philologist, critic, poet, & composer.

No man can reveal to you anything but that which already lies half-asleep in the dawning of your knowledge.

- Khalil Gibran 1883 – 1931; Lebanese artist, poet, & writer.

Is there anyone so wise as to learn by the experience of others?

- Voltaire (Francois-Marie Arouet) 1694 – 1778; French writer, historian, philosopher, & poet.

To know that we know what we know, and to know that we do not know what we do not know, that is true knowledge.

- Nicolaus Copernicus 1473 – 1543; Prussian physician, polyglot, scholar, translator, governor, diplomat, economist, astronomer, & formulated the heliocentric model of the solar system placing the Sun at the center.

Education leads to awakening then to freedom and then to evolution.

- M.I. Seka – 1972 - ; Author & businessman.

From wonder into wonder existence opens.

- Lao Tzu (Laozi) 6th century BC; Ancient Chinese philosopher.

Sell (or give) a man a fish, he eats for a day, teach a man how to fish, he eats for the rest of his life.

- (Possibly coined by Karl Marx. Often attributed to Chinese philosophers Lao Tzu 6th century BC; Chinese philosopher. (A.k.a. Laozi, circa 5th century BCE) and Confucius 551 BC – 479 BC; Chinese teacher, politician, & philosopher. Although sometimes attributed to Jesus Christ, this proverb does not exist in the Bible's New Testament.

Confucius 551 BC – 479 BC; Chinese teacher, politician, & philosopher. *Known also as **Kong Qiu**, **Zhongni**, **Kongzi**, **Kong Fuzi**, and **Master Kong**, he was an ancient Chinese philosopher and the founder of Confucianism. Confucius also strongly believed in family loyalty, respect for one's elders, morality, justice, and the golden rule of "Do not do to others what you do not want done to yourself". He died at the age of 71.*

We don't receive wisdom; we must discover it for ourselves after a journey that no one can take for us or spare us.

- Marcel Proust 1871 – 1922; French novelist, critic, & essayist.

Experience is the best teacher.

– Latin Proverb

Who questions much, shall learn much, and retain much.

- Francis Bacon 1561 – 1626; English philosopher, statesman, scientist, orator, & author.

Entire ignorance is not so terrible or extreme an evil, and is far from being the greatest of all; too much cleverness and too much learning, accompanied with ill bringing-up, are far more fatal.
- Plato 428 BC – 347 BC; Greek philosopher, mathematician, founder of Academy of Athens (the first institute of higher learning), student of Socrates & teacher of Aristotle.

Skill is better than strength.
– Polish Proverb

Experience keeps a dear school, but fools will learn in no other.
- Benjamin Franklin 1706 – 1790; American politician, One of the founding fathers of the U.S., polymath, author, postmaster, scientist, musician, inventor, statesmen, critic, & diplomat.

Falling down is how we grow. Staying down is how we die.
- Brian Vaszily; Amerian author & founder of IntenseExperiences.com.

Never read a book that is not a year old.
- Ralph Waldo Emerson 1803-1882; American lecturer, poet, & essayist.

It is difficult to get a man to understand something when his salary depends upon his not understanding it.
—Upton Sinclair 1878 – 1968; American author & Pulitzer Prize winner.

The period of greatest gain in knowledge and experience is the most difficult period in one's life.
- Dalai Lama (spiritual leader of Tibet.) The Dalai Lama is reborn over the centuries into new leaders or teachers. The current one is Tenzin Gyatso born in 1950.

The noblest pleasure is the joy of understanding.
- Leonardo da Vinci 1452 – 1519; Italian polymath, painter, sculptor, architect, musician, mathematician, engineer, inventor, geologist, anatomist, cartographer, & botanist.

In a time of drastic change it is the learners who inherit the future. The learned usually find themselves equipped to live in a world that no longer exists.
- Eric Hoffer 1902 – 1983; American writer, philosopher, & Presidential Medal of Freedom winner.

Experience is a hard teacher because she gives the test first, the lesson afterward.
- Chinese Proverb

We must continually remind students in the classroom that expression of different opinions and dissenting ideas affirms the intellectual process. We should forcefully explain that our role is not to teach them to think as we do but rather to teach them, by example, the importance of taking a stance that is rooted in rigorous engagement with the full range of ideas about a topic.
- Bell Hooks (Gloria Jean Watkins); 1952 - ; American author, feminist, & social activist.

The career of a sage is of two kinds: He is either honored by all in the world, like a flower waving its head, Or else he disappears into the silent forest.
- Lao Tzu (Laozi) 6th century BC; Ancient Chinese philosopher.

As long as people believe in absurdities they will continue to commit atrocities.
- Voltaire (Francois-Marie Arouet) 1694 – 1778; French writer, historian, philosopher, & poet.

It is difficult to beat making your living thinking and writing about subjects that matter to you.
- Eleanor Holmes Norton 1937 – American politician.

~Knowledge & Education~

Being ignorant is not so much a shame, as being unwilling to learn.
- Benjamin Franklin 1706 – 1790; American politician, One of the founding fathers of the U.S., polymath, author, postmaster, scientist, musician, inventor, statesmen, critic, & diplomat.

Most writers regard the truth as their most valuable possession, and therefore are most economical in its use.
- Mark Twain (Samuel Langhorne Clemens) 1835-1910; American author & humorist.

Thank you for sending me a copy of your book. I'll waste no time reading it.
- Moses Hadas 1900 – 1966; American teacher.

If you can't read, you can't lead.
- Leon Sullivan 1922 – 2001; American civil rights leader & minister.

Every man sees in his relatives a series of grotesque caricatures of himself.
- H. L. Mencken 1880 – 1956; American journalist, essayist, editor, critic & satirist.

There is no thief like a bad book.
- Italian proverb

Self-education is, I firmly believe, the only kind of education there is.
- Isaac Asimov (Isaak Yudovich Ozimov) 1920 – 1992; Russian American author & professor.

It often requires more courage to read some books than it does to fight a battle.
- Sutton E. Griggs 1872 – 1933; American author, minister, & civil rights activist.

Buying books would be a good thing if you could also buy the time to read them.
- Arthur Schopenhauer 1788 – 1860; German philosopher.

Either the world will destroy ignorance or ignorance will destroy the world.
- *W.E.B. (William Edward Burghardt) Du Bois 1868 – 1963; American sociologist, historian, civil rights activist, author, professor, co-founder of the NAACP & editor. Based on his statement about the U.S. rather than the world.*

He who has imagination without learning has wings but no feet.
- *French Proverb*

Nothing in the world is more dangerous than sincere ignorance and conscientious stupidity.
- *Dr. Martin Luther King, Jr. (Michael King) 1929 - 1968; American clergyman, minister, civil rights activist. Nobel Peace Prize, Presidential Medal of Freedom, & Congressional Gold Medal recipient.*

A learned blockhead is a greater blockhead than an ignorant one.
- *Benjamin Franklin 1706 – 1790; American politician, One of the founding fathers of the U.S., polymath, author, postmaster, scientist, musician, inventor, statesmen, critic, & diplomat.*

Education is our passport to the future, for tomorrow belongs to the people who prepares for it today.
- *Malcolm X (Malcolm Little) 1925 – 1965; American human & civil rights activist.*

Education is an ornament in prosperity and a refuge in adversity.
- *Aristotle 384 BC – 322 BC; Greek philosopher, polymath, & one of the fathers of Western philosophy.*

Everything that is new or uncommon raises a pleasure in the imagination, because it fills the soul with an agreeable surprise, gratifies its curiosity, and gives it an idea of which it was not before possessed.
- *Joseph Addison 1672 – 1719; English poet, playwright, essayist, & politician.*

~Knowledge & Education~

Nature is beyond all teaching. (Environment is much more important than nurture when it comes to learning.)
– *English Proverb*

A scholar who cherishes the love of comfort is not fit to be deemed a scholar.
- Lao Tzu (Laozi) 6th century BC; Ancient Chinese philosopher.

The roots of education are bitter, but the fruit is sweet.
- Aristotle 384 BC – 322 BC; Greek philosopher, polymath, & one of the fathers of Western philosophy.

A book is a gift you can open again and again.
- Garrison Keillor 1942 - ; American author, storyteller, humorist, radio personality.

When you know a thing, to hold that you know it, and when you do not know a thing, to allow that you do not know it - this is knowledge.
- Confucius 551 BC – 479 BC; Chinese teacher, politician, & philosopher.

~Leadership~

Lead, follow, or get out of the way.
- Thomas Paine 1737 – 1809; English-American author, political activist, theorist, & revolutionary.

There never was a truly great man that was not at the same time truly virtuous.
- Benjamin Franklin 1706 – 1790; American politician, One of the founding fathers of the U.S., polymath, author, postmaster, scientist, musician, inventor, statesmen, critic, & diplomat.

Far too often we become cowards when faced with individuals who have strong leadership abilities, individuals who often do not want social revolution as much as they want personal power.
- Shirley Chisholm 1924 – 2005; American politician, educator, & author.

One of the tests of leadership is the ability to recognize a problem before it becomes an emergency.
- Arnold H. Glasow 1905 – 1988; American author.

Prohibit the taking of omens, and do away with superstitious doubts. Then, until death itself comes, no calamity need be feared.
- Sun Tzu 544 BC – 496 BC; Chinese military general, strategist, & philosopher.

The best way to inspire people to superior performance is to convince them by everything you do and by your everyday attitude that you are wholeheartedly supporting them.
- Harold S. Geneen 1910 – 1997; American businessman former president of ITT Corporation.

Confidence begets confidence.

(Confidence spills over to your coworkers.)
– *German Proverb*

The best executive is the one who has sense enough to pick good men to do what he wants done, and self-restraint to keep from meddling with them while they do it.

- *Theodore (Teddy) Roosevelt, Jr.1858 – 1919; American politician, 26th President of the U.S. & Nobel Peace Prize winner.*

There is only one way... to get anybody to do anything. And that is by making the other person want to do it.

- *Dale Carnegie 1888 – 1955; American writer, lecturer, & self-improvement coach.*

The task of the leader is to get his people from where they are to where they have not been.

- *Henry Kissinger (Heinz Alfred Kissinger) 1923 - ; German American statesman, political scientist, U.S. Secretary of State, & Nobel Peace Prize recipient.*

Great leaders are almost always great simplifiers, who can cut through argument, debate, and doubt to offer a solution everybody can understand.

- *Colin Powell 1937 - ; American retired 4 star general, statesman, & 65th U.S. Secretary Of State.*

To understand the nature of the people one must be a prince, and to understand the nature of the prince, one must be of the people.

- *Niccolo Machiavelli 1469 – 1527; Italian historian, politician, diplomat, philosopher, & writer.*

Great masters merit emulation, not worship.

- *Alan Cohen 1954 - ; American businessman.*

The wicked leader is he who the people despise. The good leader is he who the people revere. The great leader is he who the people say, 'We did it ourselves.'
- Lao Tzu (Laozi) 6th century BC; Ancient Chinese philosopher.

Leadership cannot really be taught. It can only be learned.
- Harold S. Geneen 1910 – 1997; American businessman former president of ITT Corporation.

The art of leadership is saying no, not saying yes. It is very easy to say yes.
- Tony Blair 1953 - ; English politician & Prime minister.

Good management is the art of making problems so interesting and their solutions so constructive that everyone wants to get to work and deal with them.
- Paul Hawken 1946 - ; American environmentalist, entrepreneur, & author.

Leaders must be close enough to relate to others, but far enough ahead to motivate them.
- John C. (Calvin) Maxwell 1947 - ; Author, speaker, & pastor.

Leadership is unlocking people's potential to become better.
- Bill Bradley 1943 –; American politician.

Leadership is the capacity to translate vision into reality.
- Warren G. Bennis 1925 –; American scholar & author.

A leader does not deserve the name unless he is willing occasionally to stand alone.
- Henry Kissinger (Heinz Alfred Kissinger) 1923 - ; German American statesman, political scientist, U.S. Secretary of State, & Nobel Peace Prize recipient.

Be the chief but never the lord.
- Lao Tzu (Laozi) 6th century BC; Ancient Chinese philosopher.

Power is of two kinds. One is obtained by the fear of punishment and the other by acts of love. Power based on love is a thousand times more effective and permanent then the one derived from fear of punishment.
- Mahatma Gandhi (Mohandas Karamchand Gandhi) 1869 – 1948; Indian leader of Indian nationalism that used non-violent civil disobedience to lead to Indian independence.

For the strength of the Pack is the Wolf, and the strength of the Wolf is the Pack.
- Rudyard Kipling 1865 – 1936; English poet, & novelist.

Leadership is practiced not so much in words as in attitude and in actions.
- Harold S. Geneen 1910 – 1997; American businessman former president of ITT Corporation.

Benefits should be conferred gradually; and in that way they will taste better.
- Niccolo Machiavelli 1469 – 1527; Italian historian, politician, diplomat, philosopher, & writer.

I have three precious things which I hold fast and prize. The first is gentleness; the second is frugality; the third is humility, which keeps me from putting myself before others. Be gentle and you can be bold; be frugal and you can be liberal; avoid putting yourself before others and you can become a leader among men.
- Lao Tzu (Laozi) 6th century BC; Ancient Chinese philosopher.

~Leadership~

~Life-Purpose-Growth~

The price of greatness is responsibility.
- Sir Winston Churchill 1874 – 1965; British Prime Minister 1940-1945 & 1951-1955, historian, artist, & Nobel Prize winner in literature.

Sir Winston Churchill 1874 – 1965; British Prime Minister 1940-1945 & again from 1951-1955, historian, artist, & Nobel Prize winner for literature. ***Sir Winston Leonard Spencer-Churchill*** *overcame a severe lisp and stutter in order to lead England through the darkest days of WWII. He helped rally, reassure, and inspire the English populace and is widely regarded as the most influential Brit in history.*

Reading is a basic tool in the living of a good life.
- Joseph Addison 1672 – 1719; English poet, playwright, essayist, & politician.

A man's worth is no greater than his ambitions.
- Marcus Aurelius 121 AD – 180 AD; Roman Emperor, & philosopher.

Be kind, for everyone you meet is fighting a hard battle.
- Plato 428 BC – 347 BC; Greek philosopher, mathematician, founder of Academy of Athens (the first institute of higher learning), student of Socrates & teacher of Aristotle.

Perfection is attained by slow degrees; it requires the hand of time.
- Voltaire (Francois-Marie Arouet) 1694 – 1778; French writer, historian, philosopher, & poet.

One should die proudly when it is no longer possible to live proudly.
- Friedrich Nietzsche 1844 – 1900; German philosopher, philologist, critic, poet, & composer.

You are going to let the fear of poverty govern your life and your reward will be that you will eat, but you will not live.
- George Bernard Shaw 1856 – 1950; Irish playwright, co-founder of London School of Economics, critic, journalist, Nobel Prize winner, & Oscar winner.

It is better to conquer yourself than to win a thousand battles. Then the victory is yours. It cannot be taken from you, not by angels or by demons, heaven or hell.
- Buddha (Gautama Buddha) 563 BCE – 483 BCE; Nepalese (present day) sage that taught principles that Buddhism was founded on.

Out of suffering have emerged the strongest souls; the most massive characters are seared with scars.
- Khalil Gibran 1883 – 1931; Lebanese artist, poet, & writer.

In life, all good things come hard, but wisdom is the hardest to come by.
- Lucille Ball 1911 – 1989; American comedian, model, film/TV actress & studio executive.

The great man is he who does not lose his child's-heart.

- Mencius est. 372 BC – 300 BC; Chinese philosopher.

Mencius (est.) 372 BC – 300 BC; Chinese philosopher. *Also known as **Meng Ko** or **Ko**, was the most famous Confucian philosopher after Confucius himself. He argued that man by nature was good and that a lack of positive cultivating influence caused bad moral character. Others at the time were arguing that man by nature was evil.*

One time, no time -- two times, a habit.
– Swedish Proverb

The mind is everything. What you think you become.
- Buddha (Gautama Buddha) 563 BCE – 483 BCE; Nepalese (present day) sage that taught principles that Buddhism was founded on.

Ambition is the germ from which all growth of nobleness proceeds.
- Oscar Wilde 1854 – 1900; Irish writer, poet, & playwright.

The tragedy of life is not found in failure but complacency. Not in you doing too much, but doing too little. Not in you living above your means, but below your capacity. It's not failure but aiming too low, that is life's greatest tragedy.
- Benjamin E. Mays 1894 – 1984; American educator, minister, scholar, civil rights activist, & social activist.

All mankind is divided into three classes: those who are immovable, those who are movable; and those who move.
- Benjamin Franklin 1706 – 1790; American politician, One of the founding fathers of the U.S., polymath, author, postmaster, scientist, musician, inventor, statesmen, critic, & diplomat.

It is a common saying, and in everybody's mouth, that life is but a sojourn (temporary).
- Plato 428 BC – 347 BC; Greek philosopher, mathematician, founder of Academy of Athens (the first institute of higher learning), student of Socrates & teacher of Aristotle.

Revenge is a dish best served cold. (The best revenge is to live a great life. Opportunity for the second best revenge presents itself.)
– English Proverb

Life in itself is an empty canvas; it becomes whatsoever you paint on it. You can paint misery, you can paint bliss. This freedom is your glory.
– Osho (Bhagwan Shree Rajneesh) 1931 – 1990; Indian mystic, guru, professor, & spiritual teacher.

The people who get on in this world are the people who get up and look for the circumstances they want and if they can't find them, make them.
- George Bernard Shaw 1856 – 1950; Irish playwright, co-founder of London School of Economics, critic, journalist, Nobel Prize winner, & Oscar winner.

Life's gift to you is your unique vantage point. Your gift to life is expressing from it.
- Alan Cohen 1954 - ; American businessman.

Work harder on yourself than you do on your job.
- Jim Rohn 1930 – 2009; American entrepreneur, author, & motivational speaker.

Once you fully apprehend the vacuity (emptiness) of a life without struggle, you are equipped with the basic means of salvation.

- Tennessee Williams (Thomas Lanier Williams III) 1911 – 1983; American Writer, Playwright, 2 time Pulitzer Prize winner, & Poet.

Tennessee Williams (Thomas Lanier Williams III) 1911 – 1983: American Writer, Playwright, 2 time Pulitzer Prize winner, & Poet. *Having created stage classics like The Glass Menagerie, A Street car Named Desire, Cat on a Hot Tin Roof amongst others, had extraordinary success from the 1940's to the 1970's. Williams attempted to grow as a poet and playwright by attempting new things but due to his increasing alcohol and drug addiction, the quality of his work diminished considerably.*

I believe that being successful means having a balance of success stories across the many areas of your life. You can't truly be considered successful in your business life if your home life is in shambles.

- Zig Ziglar 1926 – 2012; American author & motivational speaker.

As you think, so shall you become.

–Bruce Lee 1940 - 1973; Chinese American martial artist, actor, filmmaker, & pop culture icon.

~Life-Purpose-Growth~

Golf without bunkers and hazards would be tame and monotonous. So would life.
- B. C. Forbes 1880 – 1954; Scottish-American financial journalist, author, & founder of Forbes Magazine.

It is not necessary that whilst I live I live happily; but it is necessary that so long as I live I should live honorably.
- Immanuel Kant 1724 – 1804; German philosopher.

There is a natural aristocracy among men. The grounds of this are virtue and talents.
- Thomas Jefferson 1743 – 1826; One of the founding fathers of U.S., the principal author of the Declaration of Independence, & 3rd president of U.S.

Life's Tragedy is that we get old too soon and wise too late.
- Benjamin Franklin 1706 – 1790; American politician, One of the founding fathers of the U.S., polymath, author, postmaster, scientist, musician, inventor, statesmen, critic, & diplomat.

It is best to live however one can be.
- Sophocles 497 BC – 405 BC; Ancient Greek playwright.

You have to do your own growing no matter how tall your grandfather was.
- Abraham Lincoln 1809 – 1865; American politician, 16th President of the U.S. during the American Civil war & instrumental in abolishing slavery

Don't handicap your children by making their lives easy.
- Robert A. Heinlein 1907 – 1988; American award winning science fiction writer.

Our life is what our thoughts make it.
- Marcus Aurelius 121 AD – 180 AD; Roman Emperor & philosopher.

You cannot find peace by avoiding life.
- Virginia Woolf 1882 – 1941; English writer.

Life is what you make of it. Always has been, always will be.
– English Proverb

Those who are free of resentful thoughts surely find peace.
- Buddha (Gautama Buddha) 563 BCE – 483 BCE; Nepalese (present day) sage that taught principles that Buddhism was founded on.

There are those who give with joy, and that joy is their reward.
- Khalil Gibran 1883 – 1931; Lebanese artist, poet, & writer.

Without continual growth and progress, such words as improvement, achievement, and success have no meaning.
- Benjamin Franklin 1706 – 1790; American politician, One of the founding fathers of the U.S., polymath, author, postmaster, scientist, musician, inventor, statesmen, critic, & diplomat.

Risk is a part of God's game, alike for men and nations.
- Warren Buffett 1930 - ; American Business leader, magnate, investor, & philanthropist.

The ideal man bears the accidents of life with dignity and grace, making the best of circumstances.
- Aristotle 384 BC – 322 BC; Greek philosopher, polymath, & one of the fathers of Western philosophy.

He who postpones the hour of living is like the rustic who waits for the river to run out before he crosses.
- Horace 65 BC – 8 BC; Roman poet.

There will always be some curve balls in your life. Teach your children to thrive in that adversity.
- Jeanne Moutoussamy-Ashe; Unknown.

128

All the world's a stage, and the men and women merely players. They have their exits and their entrances; and one man in his time plays many parts.

- William Shakespeare Circa 1564 – 1616; English poet, playwright, & widely regarded as the greatest English dramatist.

William Shakespeare Circa 1564 – 1616; English poet, playwright, & widely regarded as the greatest English dramatist. *Known as England's poet, who's plays have become world famous and translated into almost every language in the world.*

In life, enthusiasm and appetite are more important than anything.

- Thomas Sean Connery 1930 - ; Scottish actor, producer, Academy & Golden Globe winner.

If you want to do anything, do it now, without compromise or concession, because you have only one life.

- Gao Xingjian 1940 - ; Chinese novelist, playwright, critic, Nobel Prize in Literature winner & painter.

In each of us are places where we have never gone. Only by pressing the limits do we ever find them.
- Dr. Joyce Brothers 1927 – 2013; American psychologist, TV personality, & columnist.

Life is ten percent what happens to you and ninety percent how you respond to it.
– English Proverb

Maturity is achieved when a person postpones immediate pleasures for long-term values.
- Joshua L. Liebman 1907 – 1948; American rabbi & author.

Men have a much better time of it than women; for one thing they marry later; for another thing they die earlier.
- H.L. Mencken, American journalist, essayist, editor, satirist, critic.

The outer conditions of a person's life will always be found to reflect their inner beliefs.
- James Allen 1864 – 1912; British writer & poet.

We need a renaissance of wonder. We need to renew, in our hearts and in our souls, the deathless dream, the eternal poetry, the perennial sense that life is miracle and magic.
- E. Merrill Root 1895 – 1973; American educator & poet.

Do not think life consists of dress and show. Remember that every one's life is measured by the power that that individual has to make the world better – this is all life is.
- Booker T. (Taliaferro) Washington 1856 – 1915; American educator, orator, author, & advisor to the Presidents of the United States.

Instead of being concerned that you have no office, be concerned to think how you may fit yourself for office. Instead of being concerned that you are not known, seek to be worthy of being known.
- Confucius 551 BC – 479 BC; Chinese teacher, politician, & philosopher.

The path to our destination is not always a straight one. We go down the wrong road, we get lost, and we turn back. Maybe it doesn't matter which road we embark on. Maybe what matters is that we embark.
- Barbara Hall 1960 - ; American writer, & producer.

The height of your accomplishments is determined by the depth of your convictions.
- William F. Scolavino; Unknown.

There is only one real failure in life that is possible, and that is not to be true to the best one knows.
- John Farrar 1946 - ; Australian music producer, songwriter, singer & guitarist.

The pen that writes your life story must be held in your own hand.
- Irene C. Kasssorla; Unknown.

In the end, it's not the years in your life that count. It's the life in your years.
- Abraham Lincoln 1809 – 1865; American politician, 16th President of the U.S. during the American Civil war & instrumental in abolishing slavery.

Dig where you stand. (Bloom where you are planted. It is often best to build up upon the prowess and expertise you already have.)
– Swedish Proverb

131

Men weary as much of not doing the things they want to do as of doing the things they do not want to do.
- Eric Hoffer 1902 – 1983; American writer, philosopher, & Presidential Medal of Freedom winner.

If it doesn't feel right, don't do it. That is the lesson, and that lesson alone will save you a lot of grief.
- Oprah Gail Winfrey 1954 - ; American talk show host, actress, producer, publisher, & philanthropist.

There is more in us than we know. If we can be made to see it, perhaps, for the rest of our lives, we will be unwilling to settle for less.
- Kurt Hahn 1886 – 1974; German educator.

I'm the one that's got to die when it's time for me to die, so let me live my life the way I want to.
- Jimi Hendrix (Johnny Allen Hendrix) 1942 – 1970; American musician, singer, & songwriter.

Time is the coin of your life. It is the only coin you have, and only you can determine how it will be spent. Be careful lest you let other people spend it for you.
- Carl Bard (Carl Sandburg) 1878 – 1967; American writer, editor, & 3 time Pulitzer Prize winner.

The best way to live in this world is to live above it.
- Sonia Sanchez 1934 - ; American poet.

Enthusiasm is the most important thing in life.
- Tennessee Williams (Thomas Lanier Williams III) 1911 – 1983; American Writer, Playwright, 2 time Pulitzer Prize winner, & Poet.

A life is not important except in the impact it has on other lives.
- Jackie Robinson 1919 – 1972; American baseball player & first African American to play in Major League Baseball.

Life is full of misery, loneliness, and suffering - and it's all over much too soon.
- Woody Allen (Allan Stewart Konigsberg) 1935 - ; American comedian, screenwriter, director, actor, author, playwright, musician, & Academy Award winner.

Man cannot live without some knowledge of the purpose of life. If he can find no purpose in life, he creates one in the inevitability of death.
- Chester Himes 1909 – 1984; American writer.

I've learned that life is very tricky business: Each person needs to find what they want to do in life and not be dissuaded when people question them.
- Eli Wallach 1915 - ; American actor, Tony and Emmy Award winner.

There are only two ways to live your life. One is as though nothing is a miracle. The other is as though everything is a miracle.
- Albert Einstein 1879 – 1955; German American theoretical physicist, Nobel Prize winner, & developer of the general theory of relativity.

What allows us, as human beings, to psychologically survive life on earth, with all of its pain, drama, and challenges, is a sense of purpose and meaning.
- Barbara de Angelis 1951 - ; American relationship consultant, lecturer, author, & TV personality.

~Life-Purpose-Growth~

The wretched of the earth do not decide to become extinct; they resolve, on the contrary, to multiply: life is their weapon against life, life is all that they have.
- James A. Baldwin 1924 – 1987; American playwright, novelist, essayist, poet, critic, & civil rights activist.

Hell begins on the day when our lives grants us a clear vision of that we might have achieved, of all the gifts which we have wasted, of all that we might have done which we did not do...for me the conception of Hell lies in two words: "too late."
- Gian-Carlo Menotti 1911 – 2007; Italian American composer.

I cannot give you the formula for success, but I can give you the formula for failure, which is: Try to please everybody.
-Herbert Bayard Swope 1882 – 1958; American editor, journalist, & Pulitzer Prize recipient.

There are dreams of love, life and adventure in all of us. But we are also sadly filled with reasons why we shouldn't try. These reasons seem to protect us, but in truth they imprison us. They hold life at a distance. Life will be over sooner than we think. If we have bikes to ride and people to love, now is the time.
- Elisabeth Kubler-Ross 1926 – 2004; Swiss American psychiatrist.

What a wonderful life I've had! I only wish I'd realized it sooner.
—Colette (Sidonie-Gabrielle Colette) 1873 – 1954; French author & performer.

It isn't how long on lives, but how well. Jesus died at 33; Joan of arc at 19; Byron and Burns at 33; Marlowe at 29; Shelley at 30; Dunbar before 35....and
- Dr. Martin Luther King, Jr. (Michael King) 1929 - 1968; American clergyman, minister, civil rights activist. Nobel Peace Prize, Presidential Medal of Freedom, & Congressional Gold Medal recipient.

We have to do the best we can. This is our sacred human responsibility.
- Albert Einstein 1879 – 1955; German American theoretical physicist, Nobel Prize winner, & developer of the general theory of relativity.

Life is a grindstone, but whether it grinds you down or polishes you up depends on what you are made of.
- Robert E. Johnson 1922 – 1996; American editor, publisher, & Founder of BET.

~Love & Hate~

There is no God but Love and work is his prophet.
- W.E.B. (William Edward Burghardt) Du Bois 1868 – 1963; American sociologist, historian, civil rights activist, author, professor, co-founder of the NAACP & editor.

Woman begins by resisting a man's advances and ends by blocking his retreat.
- Oscar Wilde 1854 – 1900; Irish writer, poet, & playwright.

It is not a lack of love, but a lack of friendship that makes unhappy marriages.
- Friedrich Nietzsche 1844 – 1900; German philosopher, philologist, critic, poet, & composer.

People aren't against you, they're for themselves.
- Unknown

Marriage is the most natural state of man, and... the state in which you will find solid happiness.
- Benjamin Franklin 1706 – 1790; American politician, One of the founding fathers of the U.S., polymath, author, postmaster, scientist, musician, inventor, statesmen, critic, & diplomat.

Love cannot endure indifference. It needs to be wanted. Like a lamp, it needs to be fed out of the oil of another's heart, or its flame burns low.
- Henry Ward Beecher 1813-1887; American clergymen, speaker, & abolitionist.

Love is of all passions the strongest, for it attacks simultaneously the head, the heart and the senses.
- Lao Tzu (Laozi) 6th century BC; Ancient Chinese philosopher.

Many marriages would be better if the husband and the wife clearly understood that they are on the same side.

- Zig Ziglar 1926 – 2012; American author & motivational speaker.

I have decided to stick with love. Hate is too great a burden to bear.

- Dr. Martin Luther King, Jr. (Michael King) 1929 - 1968; American clergyman, minister, civil rights activist. Nobel Peace Prize, Presidential Medal of Freedom, & Congressional Gold Medal recipient.

Marry and grow tame.

– Polish Proverb

Where there is love there is life.

- Mahatma Gandhi (Mohandas Karamchand Gandhi) 1869 – 1948; Indian leader of Indian nationalism that used non-violent civil disobedience to lead to Indian independence.

To serve is beautiful, but only if it is done with joy and a whole heart and a free mind.

- Pearl S. Buck 1892 – 1973; American writer, novelist, Pulitzer Prize recipient, & Nobel Prize in Literature recipient.

Hatred does not cease by hatred, but only by love; this is the eternal rule.

- Buddha (Gautama Buddha) 563 BCE – 483 BCE; Nepalese (present day) sage that taught principles that Buddhism was founded on.

Do not bite at the bait of pleasure, till you know there is no hook beneath it.

- Thomas Jefferson 1743 – 1826; One of the founding fathers of U.S., the principal author of the Declaration of Independence, & 3rd president of U.S.

When you like someone, you like them in spite of their faults. When you love someone, you love them with their faults.

- Hermann Hesse 1877 - 1962; German Swill poet, novelist, & painter.

~Love & Hate~

Why hate somebody for the color of their skin when there are many better reasons?
- Denis Leary 1957 - ; American actor, comedian, writer, director, & producer.

Love is not finding someone to live with; it's finding someone whom you can't live without.
– English Proverb

The consciousness of loving and being loved brings a warmth and richness to life that nothing else can bring.
- Oscar Wilde 1854 – 1900; Irish writer, poet, & playwright.

Love can make a summer fly, or a night seem like a lifetime.
- Andrew Lloyd Webber 1948 - ; English composer, playwright, winner of several Tony and Academy Awards, & Golden globe winner.

Love... if you don't have it, no matter what else you may have, it's not enough.
- Ann Landers (Esther Pauline Lederer) 1918 – 2002; American advice columnist.

The ultimate lesson all of us have to learn is unconditional love, which includes not only others but ourselves as well.
- Elisabeth Kubler-Ross 1926 – 2004; Swiss American psychiatrist.

The door you open to give love is the very one through which love arrives.
- Alan Cohen 1954 - ; American businessman.

Love is the beauty of the soul.
- Saint Augustine (Augustine of Hippo) 354 – 430; Ancient Roman theologian, author, philosopher, & developed the idea of the central Catholic Church & original sin.

She's been married so many times she has rice marks on her face.
- Henny Youngman 1906 – 1998; English American comedian.

Love teaches even asses to dance.
- French proverb

Love's greatest gift is its ability to make everything it touches sacred.
- Barbara de Angelis 1951 - ; American relationship consultant, lecturer, author, & TV personality.

Be careful what you set your heart upon - for it will surely be yours.
- James A. Baldwin 1924 – 1987; American playwright, novelist, essayist, poet, critic, & civil rights activist.

When we feel love and kindness toward others, it not only makes others feel loved and cared for, but it helps us also to develop inner happiness and peace.
- Dalai Lama (spiritual leader of Tibet.) The Dalai Lama is reborn over the centuries into new leaders or teachers. The current one is Tenzin Gyatso born in 1950.

Let your love be like the misty rains, coming softly, but flooding the river.
- Malagasy Proverb

The most important thing in life is to learn how to give out love, and to let it come in.
- Morrie Schwartz 1916 – 1995; American sociologist professor & author.

Never get tired of doing little things for others. Sometimes, those little things occupy the biggest part of their hearts.
- Unknown

If you love somebody, let them go, for if they return, they were always yours. And if they don't, they never were.
- Khalil Gibran 1883 – 1931; Lebanese artist, poet, & writer.

Only in love are unity and duality not in conflict.
- Rabindranath Tagore 1861-1941; Bengali polymath, poet, playwright, essayist, Nobel Prize winner in literature.

~Love & Hate~

It is not beauty that endears, it's love that makes us see beauty.
- Leo Tolstoy (Count Lev Nikolayevich Tolstoy) 1828 – 1910; Russian novelist.

To love and be loved is to feel the sun from both sides.
- David Viscott 1938 – 1996; American author, psychiatrist, businessman, & media personality.

I wish I would've known more people. If I would've known more people, I would've loved more.
- Toni Morrison 1931 - ; American novelist, editor, professor, Pulitzer Prize winner, Nobel Prize recipient, & Presidential Medal of Freedom recipient.

I have found that if you love life, life will love you back.
- Arthur Rubinstein 1887 – 1982; Polish-American classical pianist.

When women love us, they forgive us everything, even our crimes; when they do not love us, they give us credit for nothing, not even our virtues.
- Honore de Balzac 1799 – 1850; French playwright & novelist.

A man in Utah is in trouble for having five wives. That's what happens in a society without alcohol, tobacco, or porn.
- Jon Stewart (Jonathan Stuart Leibowitz) 1962 - ; American political satirist, writer, director, TV host, actor, media critic, stand-up comedian, & producer.

Love is a special word, and I use it only when I mean it. You say the word too much and it becomes cheap.
- Ray Charles (Ray Charles Robinson) 1930 – 2004; American singer-songwriter, musician, & composer.

A wife lasts only for the length of the marriage, but an ex-wife is there for the rest of your life.
– Jim Samuels; Unknown.

When a girl marries she exchanges the attention of many men for the inattention of one.
- Helen Rowland 1875 – 1950; American journalist, & humorist.

It destroys one's nerves to be amiable every day to the same human being.
- Benjamin Disraeli 1804 – 1881; English politician, writer, & 2 time Prime Minister.

Love is staying up all night with a sick child or a healthy adult.
- David Frost 1939 – 2013; English journalist, comedian, writer, & TV host.

Divorce is the sacrament of adultery.
- French proverb

Love is a binding force, by which another is joined to me and cherished by myself.
- Thomas Aquinas 1225 – 1274; Italian friar, priest, philosopher & theologian.

If you find it in your heart to care for somebody else, you will have succeeded.
- Maya Angelou (Marguerite Ann Johnson) 1928 - ; American author & poet.

You never lose by loving. You always lose by holding back.
- Barbara de Angelis 1951 - ; American relationship consultant, lecturer, author, & TV personality.

Most plain girls are virtuous because of the scarcity of opportunity to be otherwise.
- Maya Angelou (Marguerite Ann Johnson) 1928 - ; American author & poet.

The greatest misfortune or happiness of man is a woman. (Choose a wife rather by your ear than your eye; a man's best fortune or his worst is a wife.)
– *French Proverb*

Love possesses not nor will it be possessed, for love is sufficient unto love.
- Khalil Gibran 1883 – 1931; Lebanese artist, poet, & writer.

~Love & Hate~

~Motivational & Inspirational~

Do the right thing.
- Spike Lee (Shelton Jackson "Spike" Lee) 1957 - ; American film director, producer, writer, & actor. Emmy and Academy Award winner.

If one advances confidently in the direction of his dreams, and endeavors to live the life which he has imagined, he will meet with a success unexpected in common hours.
- Henry David Thoreau 1817-1862; American poet, philosopher, author, abolitionist, naturalist, surveyor, & historian.

When you know what you want, and want it bad enough, you will find a way to get it.
- Jim Rohn 1930 – 2009; American entrepreneur, author, & motivational speaker.

Who seeks shall find.
- Sophocles 497 BC – 405 BC; Ancient Greek playwright.

All human actions have one or more of these seven causes: chance, nature, compulsions, habit, reason, passion, desire.
- Aristotle 384 BC – 322 BC; Greek philosopher, polymath, & one of the fathers of Western philosophy.

He that waits upon fortune, is never sure of a dinner.
- Benjamin Franklin 1706 – 1790; American politician, One of the founding fathers of the U.S., polymath, author, postmaster, scientist, musician, inventor, statesmen, critic, & diplomat.

You deserve the life you have.
- Unknown

Hunger is the best flavoring.

(Originally from Socrates)
- Greek Proverb

Socrates 469 BC – 399BC: Ancient Greek philosopher. *When the oracle at Delphi was asked "If anyone was wiser then Socrates?" The Oracles said there was not. Socrates believed he did not hold any wisdom so the Oracle must be wrong. He tested the Oracle by asking some of the wisest around of their wisdom. While these so called wise men knew a great deal, they were not wise. They in fact knew very little. Since he knew he wasn't wise and didn't hold wisdom, confirmed that the Oracle was right in the fact that the wise are aware of their lack of wisdom, while the people that claim they are wise are unaware of how much they don't know. Socrates was also credited with a method of getting to the truth or on how to solve a problem systematically, which is used today in the use of the scientific method. The development of this method is one of his greatest contributions. Socrates is also credited with being one of the founders of Western philosophy and ethics. He was forced to drink deadly poison because he would not support the political climate at the time and wanted to remain patriotic to his city-state.*

Don't worry when you are not recognized, but strive to be worthy of recognition.

- Abraham Lincoln 1809 – 1865; American politician, 16th President of the U.S. during the American Civil war & instrumental in abolishing slavery.

~Motivational & Inspirational~

Skillful pilots gain their reputation from storms and tempest.
- Epicurus 341 BC – 270 BC; Greek philosopher.

Either you run the day or the day runs you.
- Jim Rohn 1930 – 2009; American entrepreneur, author, & motivational speaker.

There is nothing in a caterpillar that tells you it's going to be a butterfly.
- Buckminster Fuller 1895 - 1983; American architect, systems theorist, author, designer, inventor, and futurist.

As the builders say, the larger stones do not lie well without the lesser.
- Plato 428 BC – 347 BC; Greek philosopher, mathematician, founder of Academy of Athens (the first institute of higher learning), student of Socrates & teacher of Aristotle.

All men are prepared to accomplish the incredible if their ideals are threatened.
- Maya Angelou (Marguerite Ann Johnson) 1928 - ; American author & poet.

I've come to believe that each of us has a personal calling that's as unique as a fingerprint - and that the best way to succeed is to discover what you love and then find a way to offer it to others in the form of service, working hard, and also allowing the energy of the universe to lead you.
- Oprah Gail Winfrey 1954 - ; American talk show host, actress, producer, publisher, & philanthropist.

Your vision will become clear only when you can look into your own heart. Who looks outside, dreams, who looks inside awakes.

- C. G. (Carl Gustav) Jung 1875 – 1961; Swiss psychiatrist & psychotherapist.

C. G. (Carl Gustav) Jung 1875 – 1961: Swiss psychiatrist & psychotherapist. *Jung was the founder of analytical psychology, developer of extraversion & introversion, archetypes, and a collective subconscious. Jung considered himself a scientist and his research included philosophy, alchemy, sociology, and literature. His work has been influential in psychiatry, study of religion, philosophy, archeology, anthropology, and literature.*

The worst thing one can do is not to try, to be aware of what one wants and not give in to it, to spend years in silent hurt wondering if something could have materialized - never knowing.

- Jim Rohn 1930 – 2009; American entrepreneur, author, & motivational speaker.

You don't look out there for God, something in the sky, you look in you.

- Alan Watts 1915 – 1973; English philosopher, writer, & speaker.

~Motivational & Inspirational~

The only sin is mediocrity.
- Martha Graham 1894 – 1991; American modern dancer, choreographer & Presidential Medal of Freedom recipient.

Where there is a will, there is a way.
(Nothing is difficult if one wants it.)
- Afghan Proverb

When you are inspired by some great purpose, some extraordinary project, all your thoughts break their bonds: Your mind transcends limitations, your consciousness expands in every direction, and you find yourself in a new, great, and wonderful world. Dormant forces, faculties and talents become alive, and you discover yourself to be a greater person by far than you ever dreamed yourself to be.
- Patanjali 500 BC - ?; Indian Yoga master.

Note how good you feel after you have encouraged someone else. No other argument is necessary to suggest that never miss the opportunity to give encouragement.
- George Burton Adams 1851 – 1925; American medievalist historian.

A thing moderately good is not so good as it ought to be. Moderation in temper is always a virtue; but moderation in principle is always a vice.
- Thomas Paine 1737 – 1809; English-American author, political activist, theorist, & revolutionary.

There is nothing more tragic than to find an individual bogged down in the length of life, devoid of depth.
- Dr. Martin Luther King, Jr. (Michael King) 1929 - 1968; American clergyman, minister, civil rights activist. Nobel Peace Prize, Presidential Medal of Freedom, & Congressional Gold Medal recipient.

~Motivational & Inspirational~

Fear less, hope more; Eat less, chew more; Whine less, breath more; Talk less, say more; Love more, and all good things will be yours!
- Swedish Proverb

Challenges are what make life interesting and overcoming them is what makes life meaningful.
- Joshua J. Marine; Unknown.

Laughter is the sun that drives winter from the human face.
- Victor Hugo 1802 – 1885; French poet, novelist, & playwright.

At bottom every man knows well enough that he is a unique being, only once on this earth; and by no extraordinary chance will such a marvelously picturesque piece of diversity in unity as he is, ever be put together a second time.
- Friedrich Nietzsche 1844 – 1900; German philosopher, philologist, critic, poet, composer.

Your vision will become clear only when you look into your heart. Those who look outside, dream. Those who look inside, awaken.
- C. G. (Carl Gustav) Jung 1875 – 1961; Swiss psychiatrist & psychotherapist.

Every day is borrowed time. You want to be able to use life as well as death as a form of service to something bigger than you; that makes life meaningful.
- Cornel West 1953 - ; American philosopher, academic, activist, author, & professor.

An invasion of armies can be resisted, but not an idea whose time has come.
- Victor Hugo 1802 – 1885; French poet, novelist, & playwright.

~Motivational & Inspirational~

The People – Could you patent the sun?
- Jonas Salk 1914 – 1995; American medical researcher, author, & virologist that discovered the polio vaccine when asked who owned the patent to his discovery.

You're alive. Do something. The directive in life, the moral imperative was so uncomplicated. It could be expressed in single words, not complete sentences. It sounded like this: Look. Listen. Choose. Act.
- Barbara Hall 1960 - ; American writer, & producer.

The first step to getting the things you want out of life is this: Decide what you want.
- Ben Stein 1944 - ; American actor, writer, lawyer, & political critic.

An amateur becomes a professional by mastering patience and perseverance.
- M.I. Seka – 1972 - ; Author & businessman.

Pain is temporary, pride is forever
- Unknown

After all these years, I am still involved in the process of self-discovery. It's better to explore life and make mistakes than to play it safe. Mistakes are part of the dues one pays for a full life.
- Sophia Loren (Sofia Villani Scicolone) 1934 - ; Italian actress.

Vision is not enough, it must be combined with venture. It is not enough to stare up the steps, we must step up the stairs.
- Vaclav Havel 1936 – 2011; Czech playwright, essayist, poet, dissident, last president of Czechoslovakia, first president of Czech Republic.

149

~Motivational & Inspirational~

Continuous effort not strength or intelligence is the key to unlocking our potential.
- Black Elk (Hehaka Sapa) 1863 – 1950; Oglala Lakota Chief.

Your living is determined not so much by what life brings to you as by the attitude you bring to life; not so much by what happens to you as by the way your mind looks at what happens.
- Khalil Gibran 1883 – 1931; Lebanese artist, poet, & writer.

There is no passion to be found playing small - in settling for a life that is less than the one you are capable of living.
- Nelson Mandela 1918 - 2013; South African anti-apartheid revolutionary & former President of South Africa, Nobel Peace Prize, Soviet Order of Lenin, and U.S. Presidential Medal of Freedom recipient.

Do more than belong: participate.
Do more than care: help.
Do more than believe: practice.
Do more than be fair: be kind.
Do more than forgive: forget.
Do more than dream: work.
- William Arthur Ward 1921 – 1994; American author.

The man who can drive himself further once the effort gets painful is the man who will win.
- Roger Bannister 1929 - ; English athlete.

Certainly the best works, and of greatest merit for the public, have proceeded from the unmarried, or childless men.
- Francis Bacon 1561 – 1626; English philosopher, statesman, scientist, orator, & author.

We will either find a way, or make one.
- Hannibal 247 BC – 182 BC; Punic Carthaginian military commander & politician.

~Motivational & Inspirational~

I do not agree with what you have to say, but I'll defend to the death your right to say it.

- Voltaire (Francois-Marie Arouet) 1694 – 1778; French writer, historian, philosopher, & poet.

Voltaire (Francois-Marie Arouet) 1694 – 1778: French writer, historian, philosopher, & poet.
Voltaire was famous for his writing and promoting freedom of religion, expression, and separation of church & state. Writing over 2000 books and essays to criticize the era's dogma's, French system of governance, and the aristocracy. He railed against the government as powerless and inept, the ruling class as parasites, the masses as ignorant and superstitious, and the church as oppressive and somewhat of a counterbalance to the monarchy. Distrusted democracy as encouraging the stupidity of the masses, since most were illiterate at the time. In his novel "Candide" he concluded, "It is up to us to cultivate our garden." Voltaire adopted his name as a mark of formal separation from his family and past.

Learn to get in touch with the silence within yourself, and know that everything in life has purpose. There are no mistakes, no coincidences. All events are blessings given to us to learn from.

- Elisabeth Kubler-Ross 1926 – 2004; Swiss American psychiatrist.

~Motivational & Inspirational~

Work is love made visible. And if you cannot work with joy but only with distaste, it is better that you should leave your work and sit at the gate of the temple, and take alms from them who work with joy.
- *Khalil Gibran 1883 – 1931; Lebanese artist, poet, & writer.*

If it fails, admit it frankly and try another. But above all, try something.
- *Franklin Delano Roosevelt (FDR) 1882 – 1945; American politician, 32nd President of the U.S., & only president to be elected for 4 terms.*

It is impossible for a people to rise above their aspirations. If we think we cannot, we almost certainly cannot. Our greatest enemy is our defeatist attitude.
- *Robert Williams 1925 – 1996; American civil rights leader.*

I believe every human has a finite number of heartbeats. I don't intend to waste any of mine.
- *Neil Armstrong 1930 – 2012; American astronaut, aerospace engineer, naval aviator, test pilot, professor, & first person to set foot on the Moon.*

What is defeat? Nothing but education; nothing but the first step to something better.
- *Wendell Phillips 1811-1884; American abolitionist, lawyer, & orator.*

Be at war with your vices, at peace with your neighbors, and let every New Year find you a better man.
- *Benjamin Franklin 1706 – 1790; American politician, One of the founding fathers of the U.S., polymath, author, postmaster, scientist, musician, inventor, statesmen, critic, & diplomat.*

I do not choose to be a common man. It is my right to be uncommon — if I can. I seek opportunity — not security. I do not wish to be a kept citizen, humbled and dulled by having the state look after me. I want to take the calculated risk; to dream and to build, to fail and to succeed. I refuse to barter incentive for a dole. I prefer the challenges of life to the guaranteed existence; the thrill of fulfillment to the stale calm of utopia. I will not trade freedom for beneficence nor my dignity for a handout. I will never cower before any master nor bend to any threat. It is my heritage to stand erect, proud and unafraid; to think and act for myself, enjoy the benefit of my creations, and to face the world boldly and say, this I have done.

- Dean Alfange 1897 – 1989; Greek-American politician.

I cannot teach anybody anything. I can only make them think.

- Socrates 469 BC – 399BC; Ancient Greek philosopher.

Life is just a chance to grow a soul.

- A. Powell Davies 1902 – 1957; American minister, author, & civil rights activist.

Build your own dreams, or someone else will hire you to build theirs.

– Farrah Gray; American businessman, investor, philanthropist, author, & motivational speaker.

Somewhere, something incredible is waiting to be known.

- Carl Sagan 1934 – 1996; American astronomer, astrophysicist, cosmologist, author, & Pulitzer Prize winner.

Begin with the end in mind.

- Stephen Covey 1932 – 2012; American educator, author, businessman, lecturer & professor.

Goals give you more than a reason to get up in the morning; they are an incentive to keep you going all day. Goals tend to tap the deeper resources and draw the best out of life.
- *Harvey Mackay 1932; American businessman & columnist.*

Only when your consciousness is totally focused on the moment you are in can you receive whatever gift, lesson, or delight that moment has to offer.
- *Barbara de Angelis 1951 - ; American relationship consultant, lecturer, author, & TV personality.*

A man knows he has found his vocation when he stops thinking about how to live, and begins to live.
- *Thomas Merton 1915 – 1968; French American writer & mystic.*

Start where you are. Use what you have. Do what you can.
- *Arthur Ashe (Arthur Robert Ashe, Jr. 1943 – 1993; American top professional Tennis player & Presidential Medal of Freedom recipient.*

Blessed is he who has found his work; let him ask no other blessedness.
- *Thomas Carlyle 1795 – 1881; Scottish philosopher, writer, historian, W satirist, & teacher.*

There are more tears shed over answered prayers than over unanswered prayers.
- *Saint Teresa of Avila 1515 – 1582; Spanish mystic, nun, writer, Catholic saint, & theologian.*

154

~Motivational & Inspirational~

Give light and people will find the way.
- Ella Baker 1903 – 1986; American civil rights & human rights activists.

What great thing would you attempt if you knew you could not fail?
- Robert H. Schuller 1926 - ; American televangelist, pastor, motivational speaker, & author.

Man is only truly great when he acts from the passions.
- Benjamin Disraeli 1804 – 1881; English politician, writer, & 2 time Prime Minister.

A man has to learn that he cannot command things, but that he can command himself; that he cannot coerce the wills of others, but that he can mold and master his own will: and things serve him who serves Truth; people seek guidance of him who is master of himself.
- James Allen 1864 – 1912; British writer & poet.

The power of imagination makes us infinite.
- John Muir 1838 – 1914; Scottish American naturalist, author, & conservationist.

The secret of getting things done is to act!
- Dante Alighieri 1265 – 1321; Italian poet & author of "Divine Comedy".

Waste no more time arguing about what a good man should be. Be one.
- Marcus Aurelius 121 AD – 180 AD; Roman Emperor, & philosopher.

To appreciate the balance in life, you have to lose it every now and then.
– Rod Williams; American musician.

~Motivational & Inspirational~

Luck is what happens when preparation meets opportunity.
- Seneca 4 BC – AD65; Roman philosopher & statesman.

Great minds have purposes, others have wishes.
- Washington Irving 1783 – 1859; American author, essayist, biographer, historian, diplomat. Authored "The Legend of Sleepy Hollow" and "Rip Van Winkle".

~Motivational & Inspirational~

~Past-Present-Future~

Time is money.
- Benjamin Franklin 1706 – 1790; American politician, One of the founding fathers of the U.S., polymath, author, postmaster, scientist, musician, inventor, statesmen, critic, & diplomat.

Each today, well-lived, makes yesterday a dream of happiness and each tomorrow a vision of hope. Look, therefore, to this one day, for it and it alone is life.
- Sanskrit poem

Have regular hours for work and play; make each day both useful and pleasant, and prove that you understand the worth of time by employing it well. Then youth will be delightful, old age will bring few regrets, and life will become a beautiful success.
- Louisa May Alcott 1832 – 1888; American novelist.

By all but the pathologically romantic, it is now recognized that this is not the age of the small man.
- John Kenneth Galbraith 1908 – 2006; Canadian American economist & diplomat.

The age we live in is a busy age; in which knowledge is rapidly advancing towards perfection.
- Jeremy Bentham 1748 – 1832; English philosopher, jurist, & social reformer.

Every new beginning comes from some other beginning's end.
- Seneca 4 BC – AD65; Roman philosopher & statesman.

One of the most tragic things I know about human nature is that all of us tend to put off living. We are all dreaming of some magical rose garden over the horizon instead of enjoying the roses that are blooming outside our windows today.
- Dale Carnegie 1888 – 1955; American writer, lecturer, & self-improvement coach.

If you love life, don't waste time, for time is what life is made up of.
- Bruce Lee 1940 - 1973; American martial artist, actor, filmmaker, & pop culture icon.

Bruce Lee 1940 – 1973: American Chinese martial artist, actor, filmmaker, & pop culture icon. *Lee was born in the San Francisco but raised in Kowloon until the age of 18 when he moved back to the U.S. to pursue a higher education. No stranger to acting or movies he elevated Hong Kong martial arts films to new levels influencing both films and the martial arts. A popular icon throughout the world, he died at the age of 32 in Kowloon Tong.*

The best thing about the future is that it comes one day at a time.
- Abraham Lincoln 1809 – 1865; American politician, 16th President of the U.S. during the American Civil war & instrumental in abolishing slavery.

There is no time like the present. (It is far better to do something now than to leave it for later, in which case it might never get done.)
- English Proverb

~Past-Present-Future~

Time will bring to light whatever is hidden; it will cover up and conceal what is now shining in splendor.
- Horace 65 BC – 8 BC; Roman poet.

Life is all memory, except for the one present moment that goes by you so quickly you hardly catch it going.
- Tennessee Williams (Thomas Lanier Williams III) 1911 – 1983; American Writer, Playwright, 2 time Pulitzer Prize winner, & Poet.

Every saint has a past and every sinner has a future.
- Oscar Wilde 1854 – 1900; Irish writer, poet, & playwright.

Never let the future disturb you. You will meet it, if you have to, with the same weapons of reason which today arm you against the present.
- Marcus Aurelius 121 AD – 180 AD; Roman Emperor & philosopher.

After a battle everyone is a general.
- Czech Proverb

You may delay, but time will not.
- Benjamin Franklin 1706 – 1790; American politician, One of the founding fathers of the U.S., polymath, author, postmaster, scientist, musician, inventor, statesmen, critic, & diplomat.

The promise given was a necessity of the past: the word broken is a necessity of the present.
- Niccolo Machiavelli 1469 – 1527; Italian historian, politician, diplomat, philosopher, & writer.

Do not dwell in the past, do not dwell in the future, concentrate the mind on the present moment.
- Buddha 563 BCE – 483 BCE; Sage that taught principles that Buddhism was founded on.

~Past-Present-Future~

If you keep chasing yesterday, you're going to miss tomorrow.
- *Unknown*

To be identified with your mind is to be trapped in time: the compulsion to live almost exclusively through memory and anticipation. This creates an endless preoccupation with past and future and an unwillingness to honor and acknowledge the present moment and allow it to be. The compulsion arises because the past gives you an identity and the future holds the promise of salvation, of fulfillment in whatever form. Both are illusions.
- *Eckhart Tolle (Ulrich Leonard Tolle) 1948 - ; German-Canadian author.*

He who has not the spirit of this age, has all the misery of it.
- *Voltaire (Francois-Marie Arouet) 1694 – 1778; French writer, historian, philosopher, & poet.*

Intolerance of your present creates your future.
- *Mike Murdock 1946 - ; American televangelist & pastor.*

A good plan violently executed right now is far better than a perfect plan executed next week.
- *George S. Patton 1885 – 1945; American general of U.S. Army of the 7th U.S. Army and 3rd U.S. Army in WWII.*

Science fiction writers foresee the inevitable, and although problems and catastrophes may be inevitable, solutions are not.
- *Isaac Asimov (Isaak Yudovich Ozimov) 1920 – 1992; Russian American author & professor.*

Maybe tomorrow's horoscope will run a correction and an apology.
- *Bill Watterson 1958 - ; American artist & author of "Calvin & Hobbes" a newspaper comic strip.*

~Past-Present-Future~

The future belongs to those who believe in the beauty of their dreams.

- *Anna Eleanor Roosevelt 1884 – 1962; Wife of Franklin D. Roosevelt, diplomat, human rights activist, first lady of the U.S. from 1933 to 1945.*

Anna Eleanor Roosevelt 1884 – 1962: Wife of Franklin D. Roosevelt, diplomat, human rights activist, first lady of the U.S. from 1933 to 1945. *Suffering through the death of both parents and a brother, Eleanor was no stranger to hardship. Even after her husband Franklin D. Roosevelt contracted Polio, she persuaded him to stay in politics going as far as giving speeches and campaigning for him. Even after FDR was elected as Governor of New York, she made public appearances for him. Held press conferences, wrote newspaper columns, spoke at national conventions, and redefined the role of the first lady. Outspoken on racial issues, women's rights, and civil rights of African American, Asian Americans, and WWII refuges. By her death she was regarded as one of the most esteemed women in the world.*

Humanity has the stars in its future, and that future is too important to be lost under the burden of juvenile folly and ignorant superstition.

- *Isaac Asimov (Isaak Yudovich Ozimov) 1920 – 1992; Russian American author & professor.*

Delayed is preferable to never. (Better late than never.)
- *Czech proverb*

I hope that when my life ends, I would have added a little beauty, perception, and quality for those who follow.
- *Jacob Lawrence 1917 – 2000; American painter.*

Rejoice in the things that are present; all else is beyond thee.
- *Michel de Montaigne 1533 – 1592; French Essayist & influential author.*

If you don't value your time, neither will others. Stop giving away your time and talents. Value what you know & start charging for it.
- *Kim Garst 1964 - ; American businesswoman.*

We are always doing something for posterity, but I would fain see posterity do something for us.
- *Joseph Addison 1672 – 1719; English poet, playwright, essayist, & politician.*

There is no future for a people who deny their past.
- *Adam Clayton Powell Jr. 1908 – 1972; American politician, & pastor.*

Never regret yesterday. Life is in you today, and you make your tomorrow.
- *L. Ron Hubbard (Lafayette Ron Hubbard) 1911 – 1986; American author & founder of Scientology.*

~Patience & Perseverance~

To begin is easy, to persist is art. (It is easy to start but hard to continue.)
- German Proverb

There is no chance, no destiny, no fate, that can hinder or control the firm resolve of a determined soul.
- Ella Wheeler Wilcox 1850 – 1919; American author, & poet.

To build may have to be the slow and laborious task of years. To destroy can be the thoughtless act of a single day.
- Sir Winston Churchill 1874 – 1965; British Prime Minister 1940-1945 & 1951-1955, historian, artist, & Nobel Prize winner in literature.

He that can have patience can have what he will.
- Benjamin Franklin 1706 – 1790; American politician, One of the founding fathers of the U.S., polymath, author, postmaster, scientist, musician, inventor, statesmen, critic, & diplomat.

The expectations of life depend upon diligence; the mechanic that would perfect his work must first sharpen his tools.
- Confucius 551 BC – 479 BC; Chinese teacher, politician, & philosopher.

A high station in life is earned by the gallantry with which appalling experiences are survived with grace.
- Tennessee Williams (Thomas Lanier Williams III) 1911 – 1983; American Writer, Playwright, 2 time Pulitzer Prize winner, & Poet.

If you want to get somewhere you have to know where you want to go and how to get there. Then never, never, never give up.
- Norman Vincent Peale 1898 – 1993; American author & minister.

Great difficulties may be surmounted by patience and perseverance.
- Abigail Adams 1744 – 1818; American wife of John Adams.
Mother of John Quincy Adams.

John Adams 1735 – 1826: American Politician, 2nd President of the U.S., a founding father of the U.S., diplomat, & first Vice President of the U.S. *A leading advocate for American independence from the British, he worked to persuade the Continental Congress to declare independence. He also assisted Thomas Jefferson in drafting the Declaration of Independence. Adams died on the 50th anniversary of the adoption of the Declaration of Independence.*

With patience you go beyond knowledge.
- Catalan Proverb

Your own resolution to success is more important than any other one thing.
- Abraham Lincoln 1809 – 1865; American politician, 16th President of the U.S. during the American Civil war & instrumental in abolishing slavery.

The general who advances without coveting fame and retreats without fearing disgrace, whose only thought is to protect his country and do good service for his sovereign, is the jewel of the kingdom.
- Sun Tzu 544 BC – 496 BC; Chinese military general, strategist, & philosopher.

Life is thickly sown with thorns, and I know no other remedy than to pass quickly through them. The longer we dwell on our misfortunes, the greater is their power to harm us.
- Voltaire (Francois-Marie Arouet) 1694 – 1778; French writer, historian, philosopher, & poet.

Giving up smoking is the easiest thing in the world. I know because I've done it thousands of times.
- Mark Twain (Samuel Langhorne Clemens) 1835-1910; American author & humorist.

Nature, time, and patience are three great physicians.
- English Proverb

The longer I live, the more I am certain that the great difference between the great and the insignificant, is energy— invincible determination—a purpose once fixed, and then death or victory.
- Sir Thomas Buxton. 1st Baronet 1786 – 1845; English politician, abolitionist, & social reformer.

Nature does not hurry, yet everything is accomplished.
- Lao Tzu (Laozi) 6th century BC; Ancient Chinese philosopher.

Morning is wiser than evening. (It's best to sleep on it.)
- Czech Proverb

~Patience & Perseverance~

Persistent people begin their success where others end in failure.
- Edward Eggleston 1837 – 1902; American historian & novelist.

To live is to suffer; to survive is to find some meaning in the suffering.
- Roberta Flack 1937 - ; American singer, songwriter, & musician.

Ralph Waldo Emerson 1803-1882: American lecturer, poet, & essayist. *Emerson led the Transcendentalist movement in the 19th century, which believed that the purity of the individual was always in danger of being corrupted by society and organized religion. He believed that self-reliance and independence was the key to human development. He advocated transcendentalism and individualism in his famous essay "Nature" in 1836. His work has influenced countless philosophers, thinkers, writers, poets, and is a central part of American thinking.*

We are made wise not by the recollection of our past, but by the responsibility for our future.
- George Bernard Shaw 1856 – 1950; Irish playwright, co-founder of London School of Economics, critic, journalist, Nobel Prize winner, & Oscar winner.

Persistence can change failure into extraordinary achievement.
- Matt Biondi 1965 - ; American Olympic gold medal winner in swimming.

The secret to success, as has been dictated throughout the ages seems to be hard work and perseverance in the direction of you passions.
- M.I. Seka 1972 - ; Businessman & Author.

There are only two options regarding commitment. You're either IN or you're OUT. There is no such thing as life in-between.
- Pat Riley 1945 - ; American former basketball coach regarded as the one of the greatest coaches of all time.

The quality of a person's life is in direct proportion to their commitment to excellence, regardless of their chosen field of endeavor.
- Vince Lombardi 1913 – 1970; American football player, & coach.

The difference between the impossible and the possible lies in a person's determination.
- Thomas Tommy Lasorda 1927 - ; American baseball player & manager.

He who knows patience knows peace.
- Chinese Proverb

Difficulties mastered are opportunities won.
- Sir Winston Churchill 1874 – 1965; British Prime Minister 1940-1945 & 1951-1955, historian, artist, & Nobel Prize winner in literature.

Adopt the pace of nature: her secret is patience.
- Ralph Waldo Emerson 1803-1882; American lecturer, poet, & essayist.

167

~Patience & Perseverance~

I believe life is a series of near misses. A lot of what we ascribe to luck is not luck at all. It's seizing the day and accepting responsibility for your future. It's seeing what other people don't see. And pursuing that vision.

- Howard Schultz 1953 - ; American businessman, founder of "Starbucks" & writer.

When the rungs were missing, I learned to jump.

- William Warfield 1920 – 2002; American singer & actor.

Patience - the gift of being able to see past the emotion.

- Rodney Williams 1959 - ; Unknown.

Celebrate the day when it is evening.

(Don't celebrate until you are 100 % sure there is a reason to do so.)

- Danish Proverb

Adversity cause some men to break; others to break records.

- William A. Ward 1921 - 1994; American author.

~Reason & Intelligence~

Prejudices are what fools use for reason.
- Voltaire (Francois-Marie Arouet) 1694 – 1778; French writer, historian, philosopher, & poet.

I am an Epicurean. I consider the genuine (not the imputed) doctrines of as containing everything rational in moral philosophy which Greek and Roman leave to us.
- Thomas Jefferson 1743 – 1826; One of the founding fathers of U.S., the principal author of the Declaration of Independence, & 3rd president of U.S.

There are three kinds of intelligence: one kind understands things for itself, the other appreciates what others can understand, the third understands neither for itself nor through others. This first kind is excellent, the second good, and the third kind useless.
- Niccolo Machiavelli 1469 – 1527; Italian historian, politician, diplomat, philosopher, & writer.

We can only reason from what is; we can reason on actualities, but not on possibilities.
- Thomas Paine 1737 – 1809; English-American author, political activist, theorist, & revolutionary.

Few people think more than two or three times a year; I have made an international reputation for myself by thinking once or twice a week.
- George Bernard Shaw 1856 – 1950; Irish playwright, co-founder of London School of Economics, critic, journalist, Nobel Prize winner, & Oscar winner.

I hear and I forget. I see and I remember. I do and I understand.
- Confucius 551 BC – 479 BC; Chinese teacher, politician, & philosopher.

I choose to live by choice, not by chance; to make changes, not excuses; to be motivated, not manipulated; to be useful, not used; to excel, not compete; I choose self-esteem, not self-pity. I choose to listen to my inner voice, not the random opinion of others...
- Unknown

The most formidable weapon against errors of every kind is reason.
- Thomas Paine 1737 – 1809; English-American author, political activist, theorist, & revolutionary.

Men use thought only as authority for their injustice, and employ speech only to conceal their thoughts.
- Voltaire (Francois-Marie Arouet) 1694 – 1778; French writer, historian, philosopher, & poet.

We are what we think. All that we are arises with our thoughts. With our thoughts, we make the world.
- Buddha (Gautama Buddha) 563 BCE – 483 BCE; Nepalese (present day) sage that taught principles that Buddhism was founded on.

The ultimate value of life depends upon awareness and the power of contemplation rather than upon mere survival.
- Aristotle 384 BC – 322 BC; Greek philosopher, polymath, & one of the fathers of Western philosophy.

New opinions are always suspected, and usually opposed, without any other reason but because they are not already common.

- John Locke 1632 – 1704; English philosopher & physician.

John Locke 1632 – 1704: English philosopher & physician. *Considered as one of the most important enlightened thinkers, his writings influenced Voltaire and many of the American revolutionaries. Some of his ideas are reflected in the U.S. Constitution and the U.S. Declaration of Independence such as "Life, Liberty, and the Pursuit of Happiness" and separation of powers. Locke believed that the self is a continuity of consciousness. He added that the mind was a blank canvas and that knowledge is determined by our experiences. His ideas were the beginning of the west's conception of the self.*

There are three things extremely hard: steel, a diamond, and to know one's self.

- Benjamin Franklin 1706 – 1790; American politician, One of the founding fathers of the U.S., polymath, author, postmaster, scientist, musician, inventor, statesmen, critic, & diplomat.

Misfortune seldom intrudes upon the wise man; his greatest and highest interests are directed by reason throughout the course of life.

- Epicurus 341 BC – 270 BC; Greek philosopher.

~Reason & Intelligence~

What is needed is not the will to believe but the will to find out, which is the exact opposite.
- Bertrand Russell 1872 – 1970; English philosopher, logician, mathematician, historian, critic, & Nobel Prize in Literature recipient.

Belief is the death of intelligence.
- Robert Anton Wilson 1932 – 2007; American author, polymath, philosopher, psychologist, essayist, editor, & poet.

The advantage of the emotions is that they lead us astray.
- Oscar Wilde 1854 – 1900; Irish writer, poet, & playwright.

Reason is God's crowning gift to man.
- Sophocles 497 BC – 405 BC; Ancient Greek playwright.

The skillful employer of men will employ the wise man, the brave man, the covetous man, and the stupid man.
- Sun Tzu 544 BC – 496 BC; Chinese military general, strategist, & philosopher.

To prefer evil to good is not in human nature; and when a man is compelled to choose one of two evils, no one will choose the greater when he might have the less.
- Plato 428 BC – 347 BC; Greek philosopher, mathematician, founder of Academy of Athens (the first institute of higher learning), student of Socrates & teacher of Aristotle.

Beware of little expenses. A small leak will sink a big ship.
- Benjamin Franklin 1706 – 1790; American politician, One of the founding fathers of the U.S., polymath, author, postmaster, scientist, musician, inventor, statesmen, critic, & diplomat.

The intelligent man finds almost everything ridiculous, the sensible man hardly anything.
– Johann Wolfang Von Goethe 1749 – 1832; German writer & politician.

~Reason & Intelligence~

The reasonable man adapts himself to the world; the unreasonable one persists in trying to adapt the world to himself. Therefore all progress depends on the unreasonable man.

- George Bernard Shaw 1856 – 1950; Irish playwright, co-founder of London School of Economics, critic, journalist, Nobel Prize winner, & Oscar winner.

George Bernard Shaw 1856 – 1950: Irish playwright, co-founder of London School of Economics, critic, journalist, Nobel Prize winner, & Oscar winner. *Shaw's writing mostly addressed social issues that were prevalent at the time mixed with comedy to make them more digestible. Religion, government, and class were his favorite themes. A strong supporter of socialism as a way to keep the working class from being exploited, he became involved with the Fabian Society and worked towards equal rights for all.*

Too clever is dumb.

- German proverb

People don't buy for logical reasons. They buy for emotional reasons.

- Zig Ziglar 1926 – 2012; American author & motivational speaker.

If past history was all there was to the game, the richest people would be librarians.

- Warren Buffett 1930 - ; American Business leader, magnate, investor, & philanthropist.

Wit is educated insolence.

- Aristotle 384 BC – 322 BC; Greek philosopher, polymath, & one of the fathers of Western philosophy.

It is better to be told "he ran then," than "he lies here". *(He who fights and runs away may live to fight another day)*
- French Proverb

Reality is that which, when you stop believing in it, doesn't go away.

- Philip K. Dick 1928 – 1982; American novelist, writer, & essayist.

It's not the load that breaks you down, it's the way you carry it.

- Lena Horne 1917 – 2010; American singer, actress, & civil rights activist.

His road of thought is what makes every man what he is.

- Zora Neale Hurston 1891 – 1960; American anthropologist, author, & folklorist.

Common sense, to most people, is nothing more than their own opinions.

- William Hazlitt 1778 – 1830; English writer, critic, & philosopher.

Let our advance worrying become advance thinking and planning.

- Sir Winston Churchill 1874 – 1965; British Prime Minister 1940-1945 & 1951-1955, historian, artist, & Nobel Prize winner in literature.

Respond intelligently even to unintelligent treatment.

- Lao Tzu (Laozi) 6th century BC; Ancient Chinese philosopher.

Learning without thought is labor lost; thought without learning is perilous.

- Confucius 551 BC – 479 BC; Chinese teacher, politician, & philosopher.

During my eighty-seven years, I have witnessed a whole succession of technological revolutions; but none of them has done away with the need for character in the individual, or the ability to think.

- Bernard Baruch 1870 – 1965; American financier, stock investor, philanthropist, & statesman.

The difference between genius and stupidity is that genius has its limits.

- Albert Einstein 1879 – 1955; German American theoretical physicist, Nobel Prize winner, & developer of the general theory of relativity.

Thoughts are the shadows of our feelings - always darker, emptier and simpler.

- Friedrich Nietzsche 1844 – 1900; German philosopher, philologist, critic, poet, & composer.

Most men seem to live according to sense rather than reason.

- Thomas Aquinas 1225 – 1274; Italian friar, priest, philosopher & theologian.

~Respect & Compassion~

Be kind whenever possible. It is always possible.
- Dalai Lama (spiritual leader of Tibet.) The Dalai Lama is reborn over the centuries into new leaders or teachers. The current one is Tenzin Gyatso born in 1950.

If you once forfeit the confidence of your fellow citizens, you can never regain their respect and esteem. You may fool all of the people some of the time; you can even fool some of the people all the time; but you can't fool all of the people all of the time.
- Abraham Lincoln 1809 – 1865; American politician, 16th President of the U.S. during the American Civil war & instrumental in abolishing slavery.

The worst sin toward our fellow creatures is not to hate them, but to be indifferent to them: that's the essence of inhumanity.
- George Bernard Shaw 1856 – 1950; Irish playwright, co-founder of London School of Economics, critic, journalist, Nobel Prize winner, & Oscar winner

Love must be as much a light, as it is a flame.
- Henry David Thoreau 1817-1862; American poet, philosopher, author, abolitionist, naturalist, surveyor, & historian.

If my survival caused another to perish, then death would be sweeter and more beloved.
- Khalil Gibran 1883 – 1931; Lebanese artist, poet, & writer.

Long live the difference (The differences
we have is what makes us interesting & unique.)
- French Proverb

176

A good man manages on his own. (Avoid being dependent on others.)
- *Swedish Proverb*

Life is never fair, and perhaps it is a good thing for most of us that it is not.
- *Oscar Wilde 1854 – 1900; Irish writer, poet, & playwright.*

I can't stand a naked light bulb, any more than I can a rude remark or a vulgar action.
- *Tennessee Williams (Thomas Lanier Williams III) 1911 – 1983; American Writer, Playwright, 2 time Pulitzer Prize winner, & Poet.*

He that displays too often his wife and his wallet is in danger of having both of them borrowed.
- *Benjamin Franklin 1706 – 1790; American politician, One of the founding fathers of the U.S., polymath, author, postmaster, scientist, musician, inventor, statesmen, critic, & diplomat.*

We all have possibilities we don't know about. We can do things we don't even dream we can do.
- *Dale Carnegie 1888 – 1955; American writer, lecturer, & self-improvement coach.*

All differences in this world are of degree, and not of kind, because oneness is the secret of everything.
- *Swami Vivekananda 1863 – 1902; Indian Hindu monk.*

Good name is better than riches. (A good name is the best of all treasures.)
- *German Proverb*

One forgives to the degree that one loves.
- *Francois de La Rochefoucauld 1613 – 1680; French author.*

~Respect & Compassion~

Morality is simply the attitude we adopt towards people whom we personally dislike.

- Oscar Wilde 1854 – 1900; Irish writer, poet, & playwright.

Oscar Wilde 1854 – 1900; Irish writer, poet, & playwright. *Born **Oscar Fingal O'Flahertie Wills Wilde** and one of London's most intelligent playwrights of his time, he is now known for his witty quotes and epigrams. Wilde left England, never to return, after being released from prison for having "unlawful relations." Wilde died in Paris, France in November 1900.*

Gratitude is the heart's memory.
- French Proverb

An eye for an eye will only serve to make the whole world blind.
- Mahatma Gandhi (Mohandas Karamchand Gandhi) 1869 – 1948; Indian leader of the Indian nationalism that used non-violent civil disobedience to lead to Indian independence.

Only a stomach that rarely feels hungry scorns common things. -
Horace 65 BC – 8 BC; Roman poet.

~Respect & Compassion~

What is the appropriate behavior for a man or a woman in the midst of this world, where each person is clinging to his piece of debris? What's the proper salutation between people as they pass each other in this flood?
- *Buddha (Gautama Buddha) 563 BCE – 483 BCE; Nepalese (present day) sage that taught principles that Buddhism was founded on.*

Men often oppose a thing merely because they have had no agency in planning it, or because it may have been planned by those whom they dislike.
- *Alexander Hamilton 1757 – 1804; American colonial politician, one of the founding fathers of the U.S., Secretary of the treasury, & statesmen.*

I have just three things to teach: simplicity, patience, compassion. These three are your greatest treasures.
- *Lao Tzu (Laozi) 6th century BC; Ancient Chinese philosopher.*

Appreciation is a wonderful thing: It makes what is excellent in others belong to us as well.
- *Voltaire (Francois-Marie Arouet) 1694 – 1778; French writer, historian, philosopher, & poet.*

He which no one envies has no fortune.
- *Spanish Proverb*

Character isn't something you were born with and can't change, like your fingerprints. It's something you weren't born with and must take responsibility for forming.
- *Jim Rohn 1930 – 2009; American entrepreneur, author, & motivational speaker.*

~Respect & Compassion~

Your net worth to the world is usually determined by what remains after your bad habits are subtracted from your good ones.

- Benjamin Franklin 1706 – 1790; American politician, One of the founding fathers of the U.S., polymath, author, postmaster, scientist, musician, inventor, statesmen, critic, & diplomat.

Fill your bowl to the brim and it will spill. Keep sharpening your knife and it will blunt.

- Lao Tzu (Laozi) 6th century BC; Ancient Chinese philosopher

There are two things a person should never be angry at, what they can help, and what they cannot.

- Plato 428 BC – 347 BC; Greek philosopher, mathematician, founder of Academy of Athens (the first institute of higher learning), student of Socrates & teacher of Aristotle.

The greatest virtues are those which are most useful to other persons.

- Aristotle 384 BC – 322 BC; Greek philosopher, polymath, & one of the fathers of Western philosophy.

Either act as you speak, or speak as you act.

- Romanian Proverb

Rather fail with honor than succeed by fraud.

- Sophocles 497 BC – 405 BC; Ancient Greek playwright.

It was character that got us out of bed, commitment that moved us into action and discipline that enabled us to follow through.

- Zig Ziglar 1926 – 2012; American author & motivational speaker.

~Respect & Compassion~

An individual has not started living until he can rise above the narrow confines of his individualistic concerns to the broader concerns of all humanity.
- *Dr. Martin Luther King, Jr. (Michael King) 1929 - 1968; American clergyman, minister, civil rights activist. Nobel Peace Prize, Presidential Medal of Freedom, & Congressional Gold Medal recipient.*

A good reputation is better than riches.
- *French Proverb*

The important thing is not how much money a person makes; it is what he does with it that matters.
- *A.G. Gaston 1892 - ; American businessman.*

Continuous effort - not strength or intelligence - is the key to unlocking our potential.
- *Sir Winston Churchill 1874 – 1965; British Prime Minister 1940-1945 & 1951-1955, historian, artist, & Nobel Prize winner in literature.*

I always pass on good advice. It is the only thing to do with it. It is never of any use to oneself.
- *Oscar Wilde 1854 – 1900; Irish writer, poet, & playwright.*

Without feelings of respect, what is there to distinguish men from beasts?
- *Confucius 551 BC – 479 BC; Chinese teacher, politician, & philosopher.*

To know oneself is to study oneself in action with another person.
- *Bruce Lee 1940 - 1973; American martial artist, actor, filmmaker, & pop culture icon.*

If you do good, good will be done to you.
(You reap what you sow.)
- *Croatian Proverb*

~Respect & Compassion~

We do not covet anything from any nation except their respect.

- Sir Winston Churchill 1874 – 1965; British Prime Minister 1940-1945 & 1951-1955, historian, artist, & Nobel Prize winner in literature.

He that would live in peace and at ease must not speak all he knows or all he sees.

- Benjamin Franklin 1706 – 1790; American politician, One of the founding fathers of the U.S., polymath, author, postmaster, scientist, musician, inventor, statesmen, critic, & diplomat.

Your pain is the breaking of the shell that encloses your understanding.

- Khalil Gibran 1883 – 1931; Lebanese artist, poet, & writer.

Everything has been thought of before by people that were smarter and richer but not better then you. The key is to do things better than they have been done before.

- M.I. Seka 1972 - ; Author & businessman.

Your silence gives consent.

- Plato 428 BC – 347 BC; Greek philosopher, mathematician, founder of Academy of Athens (the first institute of higher learning), student of Socrates & teacher of Aristotle.

The bargain that yields mutual satisfaction is the only one that is apt to be repeated.

- B. C. Forbes 1880 – 1954; Scottish-American financial journalist, author, & founder of Forbes Magazine.

Always be yourself, express yourself, have faith in yourself, do not go out and look for a successful personality and duplicate it.

- Bruce Lee 1940 - 1973; American martial artist, actor, filmmaker, & pop culture icon.

Everybody likes a compliment.

- Abraham Lincoln 1809 – 1865; American politician, 16th President of the U.S. during the American Civil war & instrumental in abolishing slavery.

~Respect & Compassion~

He that makes himself an ass must not take it ill if men ride him. (Other people will abuse you, if you let them.)
- Czech Proverb

There is no witness so terrible and no accuser so powerful as conscience which dwells within us.
- Sophocles 497 BC – 405 BC; Ancient Greek playwright.

Always recognize that human individuals are ends, and do not use them as means to your end.
- Immanuel Kant 1724 – 1804; German philosopher.

Wisdom, compassion, and courage are the three universally recognized moral qualities of men.
- Confucius 551 BC – 479 BC; Chinese teacher, politician, & philosopher.

In a controversy the instant we feel anger we have already ceased striving for the truth, and have begun striving for ourselves.
- Buddha (Gautama Buddha) 563 BCE – 483 BCE; Nepalese (present day) sage that taught principles that Buddhism was founded on.

The good man is the friend of all living things.
- Mahatma Gandhi (Mohandas Karamchand Gandhi) 1869 – 1948; Indian leader of Indian nationalism that used non-violent civil disobedience to lead to Indian independence.

Everyone knows the monkey, but the monkey knows no one. (Those that stick out are often both well-known and avoided.)
- Swedish Proverb

A man should be upright, not be kept upright.
- Marcus Aurelius 121 AD – 180 AD; Roman Emperor & philosopher.

~Respect & Compassion~

It is just like man's vanity and impertinence to call an animal dumb because it is dumb to his dull perceptions.
- Mark Twain (Samuel Langhorne Clemens) 1835-1910; American author & humorist.

Think well of everyone, but trust yourself the most. (Distrust is the mother of safety.)
- Danish Proverb

I count him braver who overcomes his desires than him who conquers his enemies; for the hardest victory is over self.
- Aristotle 384 BC – 322 BC; Greek philosopher, polymath, & one of the fathers of Western philosophy.

Good nature is worth more than knowledge, more than money, more than honor, to the persons who possess it.
- Henry Ward Beecher 1813-1887; American clergymen, speaker, & abolitionist.

It's impossible to speak what it is not noble to do.
- Sophocles 497 BC – 405 BC; Ancient Greek playwright.

To go beyond is as wrong as to fall short.
- Confucius 551 BC – 479 BC; Chinese teacher, politician, & philosopher.

Virtue is persecuted more by the wicked than it is loved by the good.
- Buddha (Gautama Buddha) 563 BCE – 483 BCE; Nepalese (present day) sage that taught principles that Buddhism was founded on.

You cannot see the brain on the forehead. (Never judge by appearances; Judge not a man and things at first sight. Things are not always as they seem, and you can not necessarily trust the evidence of your eyes.)
- German Proverb

~Respect & Compassion~

Life is creation -- self and circumstances, the raw material.
- *Dorothy M. Richardson 1873 – 1957; English author & journalist.*

The greatness of a nation can be judged by the way its animals are treated.
- *Mahatma Gandhi (Mohandas Karamchand Gandhi) 1869 – 1948; Indian leader of Indian nationalism that used non-violent civil disobedience to lead to Indian independence.*

To taste the sweet, you must taste the bitter. *(No pain, no gain; Nothing ventured, nothing gained.)*
- *French Proverb*

Obey the principles without being bound by them.
- *Bruce Lee 1940 - 1973; American martial artist, actor, filmmaker, & pop culture icon.*

He who trims himself to suit everyone will soon whittle himself away.
- *Raymond Hull 1919 – 1985; Canadian playwright & lecturer.*

Better to write for yourself and have no public, than to write for the public and have no self.
- *Cyril Connolly 1903 – 1974; English writer & critic.*

Whatever you are, be a good one.
- *Abraham Lincoln 1809 – 1865; American politician, 16th President of the U.S. during the American Civil war & instrumental in abolishing slavery.*

Let go of your attachment to being right, and suddenly your mind is more open. You're able to benefit from the unique viewpoints of others, without being crippled by your own judgment.
- *Ralph Marston 1955 - ; American writer.*

~Respect & Compassion~

Think for yourselves and let others enjoy the privilege to do so, too.
- Voltaire (Francois-Marie Arouet) 1694 – 1778; French writer, historian, philosopher, & poet.

Feeling grateful or appreciative of someone or something in your life actually attracts more of the things that you appreciate and value into your life.
- Christiane Northrup; Unknown.

Opinions founded on prejudice are always defended with the greatest violence.
- Hebrew proverb

Half of your power lies in your sameness with others. The other half lies in your uniqueness.
- Alan Cohen 1954 - ; American businessman.

Now is the moment. Act in harmony with your values, no matter what or whom you face. When you do, you will live with integrity and feel free and at peace.
- Mary Mackenzie 1922 – 1966; English actress.

It is nobler to lose honor and save the lives of men than it is to gain honor by taking them.
- David Borenstein; Unknown.

What most people need to learn in life is how to love people and use things instead of using people and loving things.
- Zelda Fitzgerald 1900 – 1948; American writer & wife of F. Scott Fitzgerald.

~Respect & Compassion~

What wisdom can you find that is greater than kindness?
- Jean-Jacques Rousseau 1712 – 1778; Genevan (currently Switzerland) writer, composer, & philosopher.

In our daily lives, we must see that it is not happiness that makes us grateful, but the gratefulness that makes us happy.
- Albert Clarke; Unknown.

If you make yourself into a doormat, people will wipe their feet on you. (Others will abuse you if you let them.)
- English Proverb

Like snowflakes, the human pattern is never cast twice.
- Alice Childress 1916 – 1994; American playwright, actor, & author.

Prejudice is a burden that confuses the past, threatens the future and renders the present inaccessible.
- Maya Angelou (Marguerite Ann Johnson) 1928 - ; American author & poet.

Love and respect are the most important aspects of parenting, and of all relationships.
- Jodie Foster (Alicia Christian Foster) 1962 - ; American actress, director, & producer.

All mankind... being all equal and independent, no one ought to harm another in his life, health, liberty or possessions.
- John Locke 1632 – 1704; English philosopher & physician.

You don't shit where you eat.
(Different segments of your life must remain separate such as business, your love life and leisure.)
- English Proverb

~Respect & Compassion~

Speaking with kindness creates confidence, thinking with kindness creates profoundness, giving with kindness creates love.
- Lao Tzu (Laozi) 6th century BC; Ancient Chinese philosopher.

Lao Tzu (Laozi) 6th century BC; Ancient Chinese philosopher. *Known by the names **Lao Tse**, **Lao Tu**, **Lao-Tsu**, **Laotze**, **Lao Tzu**, **Laosi**, and **Laocius**. Lao means "venerable" or "old" in ancient Chinese, whereas Tzu can mean both "master" and "sir". He is best known as the author of the "Tao Te Ching", making him the founder of Taoism, a pseudo-religion that teaches living in harmony with the "Tao" ("way" or "path"), which is thought to be the driving force behind everything that exists.*

Eagles don't catch flies. (People of high rank are considered – or consider themselves – too important to deal with trivial things or lowly folk.)
- French Proverb

How far that little candle throws his beams! So shines a good deed in a naughty world.
- William Shakespeare Circa 1564 – 1616; English poet, playwright, & widely regarded as the greatest English dramatist.

~Respect & Compassion~

We fear that we are inadequate, but our deepest fear is that we are powerful beyond measure.
It is our light, not our darkness, that most frightens us.
We ask ourselves: "Who am I to be brilliant, gorgeous, talented, fabulous?"
Actually, who are you not to be these things?
Your playing small doesn't serve the world.
There is nothing enlightening about shrinking so that other people around you won't feel insecure.
We are all meant to shine as children do.
It is not just in some of us; it is in everyone.
And as we let our light shine, we subconsciously give other people permission to do the same.
As we are liberated from our own fear, our presence automatically releases others.

- Marianne Williamson 1952 - ; American author, teacher, & lecturer.

It is a very delicate job to forgive a man, without lowering him in his own estimation, and yours too.

- Josh Billings (Henry Wheeler Shaw) 1818 – 1885; American humorist, writer, & lecturer.

Think of what you have rather than of what you lack. Of the things you have, select the best and then reflect how eagerly you would have sought them if you did not have them.

- Marcus Aurelius 121 AD – 180 AD; Roman Emperor, & philosopher.

~Respect & Compassion~

Take time to work - it is the price of
success
Take time to think - it is the source of
power
Take time to play - it is the secret of
perpetual youth
Take time to read - it is the fountain of
wisdom
Take time to be friendly - it is the road to
happiness
Take time to love and be loved - it is the
nourishment of the soul
Take time to share - it is too short a life
to be selfish
Take time to laugh - it is the music of the
heart
Take time to dream - it is hitching your
wagon to a star.
- *Unknown*

First deserve, then desire.
- *English Proverb*

**A person does not have to be behind
bars to be a prisoner. People can be
prisoners of their own concepts and
ideas. They can be slaves to their own
selves.**
- *Maharaji; Unknown.*

**We must learn to live together as
brothers or perish together as fools.**
- *Dr. Martin Luther King, Jr. (Michael King) 1929 - 1968;
American clergyman, minister, civil rights activist. Nobel Peace
Prize, Presidential Medal of Freedom, & Congressional Gold
Medal recipient.*

Compassion is the keen awareness of the interdependence of all things.
- *Thomas Merton 1915 – 1968; French American writer &
mystic.*

I would unite with anybody to do right and with nobody to do wrong.
- Frederick Douglas (Fredrick Augustus Washington Bailey) 1818 – 1895; American orator, writer, statesman, abolitionist, former slave, & autobiographer.

You lose a lot of time, hating people.
- Marian Anderson 1897 – 1993; American singer & civil rights activist.

Tolerance is the positive and cordial effort to understand another's beliefs, practices, and habits without necessarily sharing or accepting them.
- Joshua Loth Leibman 1907 – 1948; American rabbi & author.

Despair (hopelessness) often breeds disease.
- Sophocles 497 BC – 405 BC; Ancient Greek playwright.

A guilty conscience needs no accuser.
- English Proverb

~Respect & Compassion~

~Responsibility & The Self~

So act that your principle of action might safely be made a law for the whole world.
- Immanuel Kant 1724 – 1804; German philosopher.

The best way to keep one's word is not to give it.
- Napoleon Bonaparte 1769 – 1821; French Emperor, military & political leader.

To speak gratitude is courteous and pleasant, but to live gratitude is to touch heaven.
- Johannes A. Gaertner; Unknown.

If you know the enemy and know yourself you need not fear the results of a hundred battles.
- Sun Tzu 544 BC – 496 BC; Chinese military general, strategist, & philosopher.

Let us rise up and be thankful, for Gratitude is not only the greatest of virtues, but the parent of all the others.
- Marcus Tullius Cicero 106 BC – 43BC; Roman philosopher, politician, lawyer, orator, political theorist, consul, & constitutionalist.

Meditation takes place when you bring all your awareness to this moment.
- Brandon Bays 1953 - ; American motivational author & speaker.

Man's enemies are not demons, but human beings like himself.
- Lao Tzu (Laozi) 6th century BC; Ancient Chinese philosopher.

The real man smiles in trouble, gathers strength from distress, and grows brave by reflection.

- Thomas Paine 1737 – 1809; English-American author, political activist, theorist, & revolutionary.

Thomas Paine 1737 – 1809: English-American author, political activist, theorist, & revolutionary. *Author of the highly influential pamphlet "Common Sense", which inspired colonists in 1776 to declare independence from England. Common Sense was so influential that John Adams said that without it, there wouldn't have been a revolution. After the U.S. revolution, Pain moved to France and became involved in the French Revolution. As a defense for the French Revolution, he wrote the "Rights of Man". He was a strong advocate of reason, deism, freethinking, and argued against organized religion. Paine was voted as one of a greatest Britons in history in 2002.*

We must exchange the philosophy of excuse - what I am is beyond my control - for the philosophy of responsibility.

- Barbara Jordan 1936 – 1996; American politician, civil rights activist & Presidential Medal of Freedom recipient.

Many a man thinks he is buying pleasure, when he is really selling himself to it.

- Benjamin Franklin 1706 – 1790; American politician, One of the founding fathers of the U.S., polymath, author, postmaster, scientist, musician, inventor, statesmen, critic, & diplomat.

By failing to prepare, you are preparing to fail.
- Benjamin Franklin 1706 – 1790; American politician, One of the founding fathers of the U.S., polymath, author, postmaster, scientist, musician, inventor, statesmen, critic, & diplomat.

You are the masterpiece of your own life; you are the Michelangelo of your own life. The David that you are sculpting is you.
- Joe Vitale 1952 - ; American entrepreneur, author, & singer.

People often say that motivation doesn't last. Well, neither does bathing - that's why we recommend it daily.
- Zig Ziglar 1926 – 2012; American author & motivational speaker.

All I would tell people is to hold onto what was individual about themselves, not to allow their ambition for success to cause them to try to imitate the success of others. You've got to find it on your own terms.
- Harrison Ford 1942 - ; American film actor & producer.

We plant seeds that will flower as results in our lives, so best to remove the weeds of anger, avarice, envy and doubt...
- Dorothy Day 1897 – 1980; American journalist & social activist.

Envy and pride are the leading lines to all the misery that mankind has suffered from the beginning of the world to this day.
- John Marrant 1755 – 1791; American preacher & missionary. One of the first African-Americans to do this.

~Responsibility & The Self~

Your biggest opponent isn't the other guy. It's human nature.
- Bobby Knight 1940 - ; American retired basketball coach.

He that is good for making excuses is seldom good for anything else.
- Benjamin Franklin 1706 – 1790; American politician, One of the founding fathers of the U.S., polymath, author, postmaster, scientist, musician, inventor, statesmen, critic, & diplomat.

Men can starve from a lack of self-realization as they can from lack of bread.
- Richard Wright 1908 – 1960; American author & civil rights activist.

Character, not circumstances, make the man.
- Booker T. (Taliaferro) Washington 1856 – 1915; American educator, orator, author, & advisor to the Presidents of the United States.

When we no longer hold people responsible for their choices, civility and common sense will be diminished.
- Robert A. Levy 1941 - ; American businessman.

Anger is never without a reason, but seldom with a good one.
- Benjamin Franklin 1706 – 1790; American politician, One of the founding fathers of the U.S., polymath, author, postmaster, scientist, musician, inventor, statesmen, critic, & diplomat.

I do the very best I know how - the very best I can; and I mean to keep on doing so until the end.
- Abraham Lincoln 1809 – 1865; 16th President of the U.S. during the American Civil war & instrumental in abolishing slavery.

~Responsibility & The Self~

My life is my message.

- Mahatma Gandhi (Mohandas Karamchand Gandhi) 1869 – 1948; Indian leader of Indian nationalism that used non-violent civil disobedience to lead to Indian independence.

Mahatma Gandhi (Mohandas Karamchand Gandhi) 1869 – 1948; Indian leader of Indian nationalism that used non-violent civil disobedience to lead to Indian independence. *Gandhi's use of non-violence to fight for independence from the British has since inspired other activists around the world to use similar non-violent methods of achieving needed civil rights and freedoms. Although Gandhi had a vision of a multi-religious united India, not everyone shared in that belief. A new Muslim nationalism began forming in the early 1940s, demanding a separate Muslim homeland to be carved out of India. Due to Gandhi's support for separation of church and state, and his use of non-violence to illicit reform, he was assassinated by a Hindu nationalist in 1948.*

The time when most of you should withdraw into yourself is when you are forced to be in a crowd.

- Epicurus 341 BC – 270 BC; Greek philosopher.

A man without a purpose is like a ship without a rudder.

- Thomas Carlyle 1795 – 1881; Scottish philosopher, writer, historian, essayist, satirist, & teacher.

~Responsibility & The Self~

Know your enemy and know yourself and you can fight a hundred battles without disaster.
- *Sun Tzu 544 BC – 496 BC; Chinese military general, strategist, & philosopher.*

There are two things over which you have complete domination, authority, and control – your mind and your mouth.
- *Molefi Asante (Arthur Lee Smith, Jr.) 1942 - ; American scholar, historian, & philosopher.*

It was pride that changed angels into devils; it is humility that makes men as angels.
- *Saint Augustine (Augustine of Hippo) 354 – 430; Ancient Roman theologian, author, philosopher, & developed the idea of the central Catholic Church & original sin.*

Fear is the main source of superstition, and one of the main sources of cruelty. To conquer fear is the beginning of wisdom.
- *Bertrand Russell 1872 – 1970; English philosopher, logician, mathematician, historian, critic, & Nobel Prize in Literature recipient.*

After a period of time, the oppressed man begins imitating the behavior of the oppressor.
- *Dick Gregory 1932 - ; American comedian social activist, social critic, writer, & entrepreneur.*

If you have no confidence in self, you are twice defeated in the race of life. With confidence, you have won even before you have started.
- *Marcus Garvey 1887 – 1940; Jamaican journalist, entrepreneur, orator, publisher, & political leader.*

197

~Responsibility & The Self~

Deal with yourself as an individual worthy of respect and make everyone else deal with the same way.
- Nikki Giovanni Yolande Cornelia Giovanni Jr. 1943 - ; American writer, activist, & professor.

Millions of men have lived to fight, build palaces and boundaries, shape destinies and societies; but the compelling force of all times has been the force of originality and creation profoundly affecting the roots of human spirit.
- Ansel Adams 1902 – 1984; American photographer & environmentalist.

We are dangerous when we are not conscious of our responsibility for how we behave, think, and feel.
- Marshall Rosenberg 1934 - ; American psychologist.

The major value in life is not what you get. The major value in life is what you become.
- Jim Rohn 1930 – 2009; American entrepreneur, author, & motivational speaker.

Circumstances do not make the man, they reveal him.
- James Allen 1864 – 1912; British writer & poet.

If you don't have confidence, you'll always find a way not to win.
- Carl Lewis 1961 - ; American former track & field champion winning 10 Olympic medal (9 gold), & 10 World Championship medals (8 gold).

Only the shallow know themselves.
- Oscar Wilde 1854 – 1900; Irish writer, poet, & playwright.

In adversity remember to keep an even mind.
- Horace 65 BC – 8 BC; Roman poet.

~Responsibility & The Self~

At an early age, I started my own paper route. Once I saw how you could service people and do a good job and get paid for it, I just wanted to be the best I could be in whatever I did.
- Sean John Combs (Puff Daddy/P. Diddy) American rapper, producer, actor, & entrepreneur.

First ask yourself: What is the worst that can happen? Then prepare to accept it. Then proceed to improve on the worst.
- Dale Carnegie 1888 – 1955; American writer, lecturer, & self-improvement coach.

Old minds are like old horses; you must exercise them if you wish to keep them in working order.
- John Adams 1735 – 1826; American Politician, 2nd President of the U.S., a founding father of the U.S., diplomat, & first Vice President of the U.S.

Even were sleep is concerned, too much is a bad thing.
- Homer 7th or 8th century BC; Ancient Greek author of the Iliad and the Odyssey, poet, & orator.

Virtues are acquired through endeavor, which rests wholly upon yourself. So, to praise others for their virtues can encourage one's own efforts.
- Thomas Paine 1737 – 1809; English-American author, political activist, theorist, & revolutionary.

Who then is free? The wise man who can command himself.
- Horace 65 BC – 8 BC; Roman poet.

If one does not know to which port one is sailing, no wind is favorable.
- Seneca 4 BC – AD65; Roman philosopher & statesman.

~Responsibility & The Self~

Be gentle to all and stern with yourself.
- Saint Teresa of Avila 1515 – 1582; Spanish mystic, nun, writer, Catholic saint, & theologian.

The safest course is to do nothing against one's conscience. With this secret, we can enjoy life and have no fear from death.
- Voltaire (Francois-Marie Arouet) 1694 – 1778; French writer, historian, philosopher, & poet.

He that won't be counseled can't be helped.
- Benjamin Franklin 1706 – 1790; American politician, One of the founding fathers of the U.S., polymath, author, postmaster, scientist, musician, inventor, statesmen, critic, & diplomat.

There is no greater agony than bearing an untold story inside you.
- Maya Angelou (Marguerite Ann Johnson) 1928 - ; American author & poet.

A portion of mankind take pride in their vices and pursue their purpose; many more waver between doing what is right and complying with what is wrong.
- Horace 65 BC – 8 BC; Roman poet.

There are slavish souls who carry their appreciation for favors done them so far that they strangle themselves with the rope of gratitude.
- Friedrich Nietzsche 1844 – 1900; German philosopher, philologist, critic, poet, & composer.

I am not what happened to me, I am what I choose to become...
- C. G. (Carl Gustav) Jung 1875 – 1961; Swiss psychiatrist & psychotherapist.

~Responsibility & The Self~

Choose a subject equal to your abilities; think carefully what your shoulders may refuse, and what they are capable of bearing.
- Horace 65 BC – 8 BC; Roman poet.

Having been poor is no shame, but being ashamed of it, is.
- Benjamin Franklin 1706 – 1790; American politician, One of the founding fathers of the U.S., polymath, author, postmaster, scientist, musician, inventor, statesmen, critic, & diplomat.

For people that have discovered themselves and their purpose, there isn't enough time. For people that haven't begun to live, there is too much time.
- M.I. Seka 1972 - ; Author & businessman.

We all start out as children.
(Mistakes should be expected of beginners.)
- Swedish Proverb

There is a criterion by which you can judge whether the thoughts you are thinking and the things you are doing are right for you. The criterion is: Have they brought you inner peace?
- Peace Pilgrim (Mildred Norman Ryder) 1908 – 1981; American spiritual teacher, mystic, pacifist, vegetarian activist, & peace activist.

He that composes himself is wiser than he that composes a book.
- Benjamin Franklin 1706 – 1790; American politician, One of the founding fathers of the U.S., polymath, author, postmaster, scientist, musician, inventor, statesmen, critic, & diplomat.

It is better to do one's own duty, however defective it may be, than to follow the duty of another, however well one may perform it. He who does his duty as his own nature reveals it, never sins.
- Lao Tzu (Laozi) 6th century BC; Ancient Chinese philosopher.

~Responsibility & The Self~

If you can't get a compliment any other way, pay yourself one.
- Mark Twain (Samuel Langhorne Clemens) 1835-1910; American author & humorist.

To have a great man for a friend seems pleasant to those who have never tried it; those who have, fear it.
- Horace 65 BC – 8 BC; Roman poet.

Silence is a source of great strength.
- Lao Tzu (Laozi) 6th century BC; Ancient Chinese philosopher.
If your ship doesn't come in, swim out to it.
- Jonathan Winters 1925 – 2013; American comedian, actor, author, Grammy Award winner, & artist

~Science~

If history and science have taught us anything, it is that passion and desire are not the same as truth.
- E. O. (Edward Osborn) Wilson 1929 - ; American biologist, researcher, theorist, naturalist, & author.

The virtues of science are skepticism and independence of thought.
- Walter Gilbert 1932 - ; American physicist, biochemist, molecular biologist, & Nobel Prize in Chemistry recipient.

Science has done more for the development of western civilization in one hundred years than Christianity did in eighteen hundred years.
- John Burroughs 1837 – 1921; American naturalist & essayist.

The man of science has learned to believe in justification, not by faith, but by verification.
- Thomas Henry Huxley 1825 – 1895; English biologist.

Science is wonderfully equipped to answer the question 'How?' but it gets terribly confused when you ask the question 'Why?'
- Erwin Chargaff 1905 – 2002; Austrian American biochemist.

The whole history of science has been the gradual realization that events do not happen in an arbitrary manner, but that they reflect a certain underlying order, which may or may not be divinely inspired.
- Stephen Hawking 1942 - ; English theoretical physicist, cosmologist, author, & Director of Research at University of Cambridge.

Reason, observation, and experience; the holy trinity of science.

- Robert Green Ingersoll 1833 – 1899; American Civil war veteran, political leader, & noted agnostic.

Robert Green Ingersoll 1833 – 1899: American Civil war veteran, political leader, & noted agnostic. *A lawyer by trade, Ingersoll was a gifted orator giving speeches, which was part of public entertainment at the time on various subjects. His most popular was on agnosticism. Advocating free thought and humanism against organized religious beliefs, which caused him to be a target of the press.*

There is one thing even more vital to science than intelligent methods; and that is, the sincere desire to find out the truth, whatever it may be.

- Charles Pierce 1926 – 1999; American entertainer.

Scientists have become the bearers of the torch of discovery in our quest for knowledge.

- Stephen Hawking 1942 - ; English theoretical physicist, cosmologist, author, & Director of Research at University of Cambridge.

Science is the father of knowledge, but opinion breeds ignorance.
- Hippocrates of Kos 460 BC – 370 BC; Ancient Greek physician considered the father of western medicine.

The scientist is motivated primarily by curiosity and a desire for truth.
- Irving Langmuir 1881 – 1957; American chemist & physicist.

Not only does God play dice, but... he sometimes throws them where they cannot be seen.
- Stephen Hawking 1942 - ; English theoretical physicist, cosmologist, author, & Director of Research at University of Cambridge.

It is surely harmful to souls to make it a heresy to believe what is proved.
- Galileo Galilei 1564 – 1642; Italian physicist, mathematician, astronomer, & philosopher & polymath.

It has become part of the accepted wisdom to say that the twentieth century was the century of physics and the twenty-first century will be the century of biology.
- Freeman Dyson 1823 - ; English American theoretical physicist & mathematician.

I would like nuclear fusion to become a practical power source. It would provide an inexhaustible supply of energy, without pollution or global warming.
- Stephen Hawking 1942 - ; English theoretical physicist, cosmologist, author, & Director of Research at University of Cambridge.

~Society-Community-Cooperation~

We have it in our power to begin the world over again.

- Thomas Paine 1737 – 1809; English-American author, political activist, theorist, & revolutionary.

The disgrace of others often keeps tender minds from vice.

- Horace 65 BC – 8 BC; Roman poet.

Froth at the top, dregs at bottom, but the middle excellent.

- Voltaire (Francois-Marie Arouet) 1694 – 1778; French writer, historian, philosopher, & poet.

When a hundred men stand together, each of them loses his mind and gets another one.

- Friedrich Nietzsche 1844 – 1900; German philosopher, philologist, critic, poet, & composer.

If God listened to the prayers of men, all men would quickly have perished: for they are forever praying for evil against one another.

- Epicurus 341 BC – 270 BC; Greek philosopher.

Whenever you find yourself on the side of the majority, it is time to pause and reflect.

- Mark Twain (Samuel Langhorne Clemens) 1835-1910; American author & humorist.

Greatness lies, not in being strong, but in the right using of strength; and strength is not used rightly when it serves only to carry a man above his fellows for his own solitary glory. He is the greatest whose strength carries up the most hearts by the attraction of his own.

- Henry Ward Beecher 1813-1887; American clergymen, speaker, & abolitionist.

Henry Ward Beecher 1813-1887: American clergymen, speaker, & abolitionist. *Brother of Harriet Beecher Stowe who was the author of "Uncle Tom's Cabin" was a gifted orator, which he used to emphasize God's love, abolitionism, women's suffrage, temperance, and the theory of evolution.*

The worst wheel of the cart makes the most noise.

- Benjamin Franklin 1706 – 1790; American politician, One of the founding fathers of the U.S., polymath, author, postmaster, scientist, musician, inventor, statesmen, critic, & diplomat.

United we stand, divided we fall; Union is strength.

- Croatian Proverb

The books that the world calls immoral are books that show the world its own shame.
- Oscar Wilde 1854 – 1900; Irish writer, poet, & playwright.

Patriotism is the conviction that your country is superior to all others because you were born in it.
- George Bernard Shaw 1856 – 1950; Irish playwright, co-founder of London School of Economics, critic, journalist, Nobel Prize winner, & Oscar winner.

Nothing can be more absurd than the practice that prevails in our country of men and women not following the same pursuits with all their strengths and with one mind, for thus, the state instead of being whole is reduced to half.
- Plato 428 BC – 347 BC; Greek philosopher, mathematician, founder of Academy of Athens (the first institute of higher learning), student of Socrates & teacher of Aristotle.

A free life cannot acquire many possessions, because this is not easy to do without servility to mobs or monarchs.
- Epicurus 341 BC – 270 BC; Greek philosopher.

If you can dream it, then you can achieve it. You will get all you want in life if you help enough other people get what they want.
- Zig Ziglar 1926 – 2012; American author & motivational speaker.

Morality is the herd-instinct in the individual.
- Friedrich Nietzsche 1844 – 1900; German philosopher, philologist, critic, poet, & composer.

Educate and inform the whole mass of the people... They are the only sure reliance for the preservation of our liberty.
- Thomas Jefferson 1743 – 1826; One of the founding fathers of U.S., the principal author.

The best way to help people is to make it possible for them to help themselves.
- M.I. Seka 1972 - ; Author & businessman.

When a nation is filled with strife, then do patriots flourish.
- Lao Tzu (Laozi) 6th century BC; Ancient Chinese philosopher.

Democracy is a form of government that substitutes election by the incompetent many for appointment by the corrupt few.
- George Bernard Shaw 1856 – 1950; Irish playwright, co-founder of London School of Economics, critic, journalist, Nobel Prize winner, & Oscar winner.

The envious man grows lean at the success of his neighbor.
- Horace 65 BC – 8 BC; Roman poet.

The ancient Romans built their greatest masterpieces of architecture, their amphitheaters, for wild beasts to fight in.
- Voltaire (Francois-Marie Arouet) 1694 – 1778; French writer, historian, philosopher, & poet.

The youth need to be enabled to become job generators from job seekers.
- Abdul Kalam 1931; Indian scientist, & 11th president of India.

I suppose society is wonderfully delightful. To be in it is merely a bore. But to be out of it is simply a tragedy.
- Oscar Wilde 1854 – 1900; Irish writer, poet, & playwright.

Eat to please thyself, but dress to please others.
- Benjamin Franklin 1706 – 1790; American politician, One of the founding fathers of the U.S., polymath, author, postmaster, scientist, musician, inventor, statesmen, critic, & diplomat.

The sage does not hoard. The more he helps others, the more he benefits himself, the more he gives to others, the more he gets himself. The Way of Heaven does one good but never does one harm. The Way of the sage is to act but not to compete.
- Lao Tzu (Laozi) 6th century BC; Ancient Chinese philosopher.

Statistics suggest that when customers complain, business owners and managers ought to get excited about it. The complaining customer represents a huge opportunity for more business.
- Zig Ziglar 1926 – 2012; American author & motivational speaker.

I am not bound to win, but I am bound to be true. I am not bound to succeed, but I am bound to live by the light that I have. I must stand with anybody that stands right, and stand with him while he is right, and part with him when he goes wrong.
- Abraham Lincoln 1809 – 1865; American politician, 16th President of the U.S. during the American Civil war & instrumental in abolishing slavery.

The natural progress of things is for liberty to yield and government to gain ground.
- Thomas Jefferson 1743 – 1826; One of the founding fathers of America, the principal author of the Declaration of Independence, 3rd president of U.S.

There is no harm in repeating a good thing.

- Plato 428 BC – 347 BC; Greek philosopher, mathematician, founder of Academy of Athens (the first institute of higher learning), student of Socrates & teacher of Aristotle.

Where liberty is, there is my country.

- Benjamin Franklin 1706 – 1790; American politician, One of the founding fathers of the U.S., polymath, author, postmaster, scientist, musician, inventor, statesmen, critic, & diplomat.

Benjamin Franklin 1706 – 1790; American politician, One of the founding fathers of the U.S., polymath, author, postmaster, scientist, musician, inventor, statesmen, critic, & diplomat. *Some of Franklin's accomplishments are difficult to believe, such as the fact that he was a scientist who played a major role in the American enlightenment. He discovered electricity and formulated various theories regarding it, invented the lightning rod, bifocals, odometer, and the "Franklin stove." He was one of the first proponents for colonial unity earning him the title: "The First American." Towards the end of his life, Franklin freed his slaves and became a prominent abolitionist. His extraordinary life is honored not only on U.S. currency, but also in the names of warships, towns, counties, educational institutions, and companies.*

Sticks in a bundle are unbreakable.

- Kenyan Proverb

All that is necessary for evil to succeed is for good men to do nothing.

- Edmund Burke 1729 – 1797; Irish statesman, author, & philosopher.

We are all dependent on one another, every soul of us on earth.

- George Bernard Shaw 1856 – 1950; Irish playwright, co-founder of London School of Economics, critic, journalist, Nobel Prize winner, & Oscar winner.

Someone's sitting in the shade today because someone planted a tree a long time ago.

- Warren Buffett 1930 - ; American Business leader, magnate, investor, & philanthropist.

Who is wise? He that learns from everyone. Who is powerful? He that governs his passions. Who is rich? He that is content. Who is that? Nobody.

- Benjamin Franklin 1706 – 1790; American politician, One of the founding fathers of the U.S., polymath, author, postmaster, scientist, musician, inventor, statesmen, critic, & diplomat.

In almost any society, I think, the quality of the nonconformist is likely to be Just as good, and no better than, that of the conformists.

- Margaret Mead 1901 – 1978; American cultural anthropologist.

For civilization to make progress, each generation has to do better than the last one.

- Hector Ruiz 1945 - ; Mexican American businessman.

You can stand tall without standing on someone. You can be a victor without having victims.

- Harriet Woods 1927 – 2007; American politician.

A man is as faithful as his options.
- Bill Maher 1956 - ; American stand-up comedian, TV host, political commentator, satirist, author, & actor.

Nothing so needs reforming as other people's habits.
- Mark Twain (Samuel Langhorne Clemens) 1835-1910; American author & humorist.

Safeguarding the rights of others is the most noble and beautiful end of a human being.
- Khalil Gibran 1883 – 1931; Lebanese artist, poet, & writer.

True humor is fun - it does not put down, kid, or mock. It makes people feel wonderful, not separate, different, and cut off. True humor has beneath it the understanding that we are all in this together.
- Hugh Prather 1938 – 2010; American writer, minster, & counselor.

Law and order exist for the purpose of establishing justice and when they fail in this purpose they become the dangerously structured dams that block the flow of social progress.
- Dr. Martin Luther King, Jr. (Michael King) 1929 - 1968; American clergyman, minister, civil rights activist. Nobel Peace Prize, Presidential Medal of Freedom, & Congressional Gold Medal recipient.

We don't bump into every neighbor, so a lot of wisdom never gets passed on.
- Candy Chang 1989 - ; Chinese actress.

Gentleness, self-sacrifice and generosity are the exclusive possession of no one race or religion.
- Mahatma Gandhi (Mohandas Karamchand Gandhi) 1869 – 1948; Indian leader of Indian nationalism that used non-violent civil disobedience to lead to Indian independence.

Life's most persistent and urgent question is, what are you doing for others?

- Dr. Dr. Martin Luther King, Jr. (Michael King) 1929 - 1968; American clergyman, minister, civil rights activist. Nobel Peace Prize, Presidential Medal of Freedom, & Congressional Gold Medal recipient.

Dr. Martin Luther King, Jr. (Michael King) 1929 - 1968; American clergyman, minister, civil rights activist, as well as the recipient of the Nobel Peace Prize, Presidential Medal of Freedom, & the Congressional Gold Medal. *To say that Dr. King was just a civil rights activist would do him injustice. Dr. King changed the course of history in the United States and in the world. A Baptist minister turned civil rights activist, who was originally skeptical of many of Christian doctrines, only later in life did Dr. King conclude the Bible had many other profound truths. Dr. King received a B.A. in sociology in 1948 and his Ph.D. in 1955. He was heavily influenced by the non-violent teachings of Jesus Christ that said: "love your neighbor as yourself", "love your enemies", and "love God above all." Inspired by Mahatma Gandhi's non-violence activism, which, in turn, was inspired by Russian anarchist Leo Tolstoy, as well as forward thinkers such as Thoreau, Dr. King organized the 1955 Montgomery Bus boycott and the non-violent Birmingham protests of 1962. In 1963, Dr. King help organize the March on Washington, where he delivered his famous "I Have a Dream" speech, which became regarded as one of the finest speeches in American history. Dr. King helped put*

~Society-Community-Cooperation~

civil rights at the top of the political agenda and facilitated the passage of the Civil Rights Act of 1964. Dr. King was assassinated in Memphis, Tennessee in 1968.

Don't be afraid of the dog who barks, but be afraid of the one, who is silent and wags its tail. (It's the quiet ones you got to watch.)
- Russian Proverb

How much time he saves who does not look to see what his neighbor says or does or thinks.
- Marcus Aurelius 121 AD – 180 AD; Roman Emperor & philosopher.

If you once forfeit the confidence of your fellow citizens, you can never regain their respect and esteem. You may fool all of the people some of the time; you can even fool some of the people all the time; but you can't fool all of the people all of the time.
- Abraham Lincoln 1809 – 1865; American politician, 16th President of the U.S. during the American Civil war & instrumental in abolishing slavery.

The most perfect political community is one in which the middle class is in control, and outnumbers both of the other classes.
- Aristotle 384 BC – 322 BC; Greek philosopher, polymath, & one of the fathers of Western philosophy.

Successful people are always looking for opportunities to help others. Unsuccessful people are always asking, "What's in it for me?
- Brian Tracy 1944 - ; Canadian motivational speaker & author.

It is by acts and not by ideas that people live.
- Harry Emerson Fosdick 1878 – 1969; American pastor.

Where a man can live, he can also live well.
- Marcus Aurelius 121 AD – 180 AD; Roman Emperor, & philosopher.

Don't put out a fire that isn't burning
you. (Mind your own business. Don't get involved into other peoples' problems).
- Czech Proverb

Of all the varieties of virtues, liberalism is the most beloved.
- Aristotle 384 BC – 322 BC; Greek philosopher, polymath, & one of the fathers of Western philosophy.

An individual has not started living until he can rise above the narrow confines of his individualistic concerns to the broader concerns of all humanity.
- Dr. Martin Luther King, Jr. (Michael King) 1929 - 1968; American clergyman, minister, civil rights activist. Nobel Peace Prize, Presidential Medal of Freedom, & Congressional Gold Medal recipient.

Remember, if you ever need a helping hand, it's at the end of your arm. As you get older, remember you have another hand: The first is to help yourself; the second is to help others.
- Audrey Hepburn (Audrey Kathleen Ruston) 1929 – 1993; British actress, humanitarian. Academy, Emmy, Golden Globe, Grammy, Tony, and Screen Actors guild award winner.

It is necessary for him who lays out a state and arranges laws for it to presuppose that all men are evil and that they are always going to act according to the wickedness of their spirits whenever they have free scope.
- Niccolo Machiavelli 1469 – 1527; Italian historian, politician, diplomat, philosopher, & writer.

Hands that serve are holier than lips that pray.
- Sai Baba (Shirdi Sai Baba) ? – 1918; Indian guru, yogi, & fakir.

~Society-Community-Cooperation~

So powerful is the light of unity that it can illuminate the whole earth.
- Bahaullah (Mirza Husayn-Ali Nuri) 1817 – 1892; Persian (modern day Iran) founder of the Bahai faith.

No matter what accomplishments you make, somebody helps you.
- Althea Gibson 1927 – 2003; American tennis player & professional golfer.

No people come into possession of a culture without having paid a heavy price for it.
- James A. Baldwin 1924 – 1987; American playwright, novelist, essayist, poet, critic, & civil rights activist.

If we live good lives, the times are also good. As we are, such are the times.
- Saint Augustine (Augustine of Hippo) 354 – 430; Ancient Roman theologian, author, philosopher, & developed the idea of the central Catholic Church & original sin.

A great city is not to be confounded with a populous one.
- Aristotle 384 BC – 322 BC; Greek philosopher, polymath, & one of the fathers of Western philosophy.

Shared joy is a double joy; shared sorrow is half sorrow.
- Swedish Proverb

He who stands aloof runs the risk of believing himself better than others and misusing his critique of society as an ideology for his private interest.
- Theodor Adorno 1903 – 1969; German sociologist, philosopher, musicologist, & critic.

The tendency in modern civilization is to make the world uniform... Let the mind be universal. The individual should not be sacrificed.
- Rabindranath Tagore 1861-1941; Bengali polymath, poet, playwright, essayist, Nobel Prize winner in literature.

It is only as we develop others that we permanently succeed.
- Harvey S. Firestone 1868 – 1938; American businessman.

Not only is the self-entwined in society; it owes society its existence in the most literal sense.
- Theodor Adorno 1903 – 1969; German sociologist, philosopher, musicologist, & critic.

One meets/greets people by their clothes, and says farewell by their mind.
(Beauty may open the door, but only virtue enters.)
- Russian Proverb

Everybody laughs the same in every language because laughter is a universal connection.
- Yakov Smirnoff 1951 - ; Ukrainian American comedian & professor.

A small body of determined spirits fired by an unquenchable faith in their mission can alter the course of history.
- Mahatma Gandhi (Mohandas Karamchand Gandhi) 1869 – 1948; Indian leader of Indian nationalism that used non-violent civil disobedience to lead to Indian independence.

At his best, man is the noblest of all animals; separated from law and justice he is the worst.
- Aristotle 384 BC – 322 BC; Greek philosopher, polymath, & one of the fathers of Western philosophy.

Don't ask yourself what the world needs; ask yourself what makes you come alive. And then go and do that. Because what the world needs is people who have come alive.
- Howard Thurman 1899 – 1981; American author, philosopher, theologian, educator, & civil rights leader.

Alone we can do so little; together we can do so much.
- Helen Adams Keller 1880 – 1968; American author, political activist, first deaf-blind person to earn a B.A. & lecturer.

Only a humanity to whom death has become as indifferent as its members, that has itself died, can inflict it administratively on innumerable people.
- Theodor Adorno 1903 – 1969; German sociologist, philosopher, musicologist, & critic.

That which is not good for the bee-hive cannot be good for the bees.
- Marcus Aurelius 121 AD – 180 AD; Roman Emperor, & philosopher.

The hardest hit, as everywhere, are those who have no choice.
- Theodor Adorno 1903 – 1969; German sociologist, philosopher, musicologist, & critic.

~Success & Failure~

Don't be afraid to give your best to what seemingly are small jobs. Every time you conquer one it makes you that much stronger. If you do the little jobs well, the big ones will tend to take care of themselves.
- Dale Carnegie 1888 – 1955; American writer, lecturer, & self-improvement coach.

Let others lead small lives, but not you. Let others argue over small things, but not you. Let others cry over small hurts, but not you. Let others leave their future in someone else's hands, but not you.
- Jim Rohn 1930 – 2009; American entrepreneur, author, & motivational speaker.

It's a good thing to be foolishly gay once in a while.
- Horace 65 BC – 8 BC; Roman poet.

I assess the power of a will by how much resistance, pain, torture it endures and knows how to turn to its advantage.
- Friedrich Nietzsche 1844 – 1900; German philosopher, philologist, critic, poet, & composer.

People in their handlings of affairs often fail when they are about to succeed. If one remains as careful at the end as he was at the beginning, there will be no failure.
- Lao Tzu (Laozi) 6th century BC; Ancient Chinese philosopher.

If you want to be successful, it's just this simple. Know what you are doing. Love what you are doing. And believe in what you are doing.

- Will Rogers 1879 – 1935; American humorist, social commentator, actor, & writer.

Will Rogers 1879 – 1935; American humorist, social commentator, actor, & writer. *Born* ***William Penn Adair Rogers*** *in Indian Territory now known as Oklahoma, became one of the most famous social commentators in the 1920s and 1930s. His folksy and simplistic social comments allowed him to mock everyone from gangsters to politician without causing offense. He even ran for President in 1928, campaigning solely through the pages of Life Magazine. His only promise was that if elected, he would resign immediately. Although he didn't win, on Election Day, he declared victory and promptly resigned. Rogers was admired for his views of the "common man" in America, his individualism, democratic ideas, and liberal philosophies. He was an ardent supporter of hard work, long hours, the self-made man, progress, and the American dream of achieving success. Rogers died in a plane crash in Alaska in 1935.*

I'll either find a way or make one.

- Latin Proverb

Secret operations are essential in war; upon them the army relies to make its every move.
- Sun Tzu 544 BC – 496 BC; Chinese military general, strategist, & philosopher.

Performance is your reality. Forget everything else.
- Harold S. Geneen 1910 – 1997; American businessman former president of ITT Corporation.

When it is obvious that the goals cannot be reached, don't adjust the goals, adjust the action steps.
- Confucius 551 BC – 479 BC; Chinese teacher, politician, & philosopher.

Fast is fine, but accuracy is everything.
- Xenophon 430 BC – 354 BC; Ancient Greek historian, soldier, mercenary, & philosopher.

Discipline is the bridge between goals and accomplishment.
- Jim Rohn 1930 – 2009; American entrepreneur, author, & motivational speaker.

Success is the maximum utilization of the ability that you have.
- Zig Ziglar 1926 – 2012; American author & motivational speaker.

Whosoever desires constant success must change his conduct with the times.
- Niccolo Machiavelli 1469 – 1527; Italian historian, politician, diplomat, philosopher, & writer.

Give me six hours to chop down a tree and I will spend the first four sharpening the axe.
- Abraham Lincoln 1809 – 1865; American politician, 16th President of the U.S. during the American Civil war & instrumental in abolishing slavery.

~Success & Failure~

The man who makes everything that leads to happiness depends upon himself, and not upon other men, has adopted the very best plan for living happily. This is the man of moderation, the man of manly character and of wisdom.

- Plato 428 BC – 347 BC; Greek philosopher, mathematician, founder of Academy of Athens (the first institute of higher learning), student of Socrates & teacher of Aristotle.

It is not enough to succeed. Others must fail.

- Gore Vidal 1925 – 2012; American writer, critic, & humorist.

Failure is not a single, cataclysmic event. You don't fail overnight. Instead, failure is a few errors in judgment, repeated every day.

- Jim Rohn 1930 – 2009; American entrepreneur, author, & motivational speaker.

The general who wins the battle makes many calculations in his temple before the battle is fought. The general who loses makes but few calculations beforehand.

- Sun Tzu 544 BC – 496 BC; Chinese military general, strategist, & philosopher.

The man who has done his level best... is a success, even though the world may write him down a failure.

- B. C. Forbes 1880 – 1954; Scottish-American financial journalist, author, & founder of Forbes Magazine.

So long as there is breath in me, that long I will persist. For now I know one of the greatest principles on success; if I persist long enough I will win.

- Augustine "Og" Mandino II 1923 – 1996; American author.

When fate hands you a lemon, make lemonade.
- Dale Carnegie 1888 – 1955; American writer, lecturer, & self-improvement coach.

If you want to succeed you should strike out on new paths, rather than travel the worn paths of accepted success.
- John D. Rockefeller 1839 – 1937; American industrialist & philanthropist.

Failure is simply a few errors in judgment, repeated every day.
- Jim Rohn 1930 – 2009; American entrepreneur, author, & motivational speaker.

**Anticipate the difficult
The five essential entrepreneurial skills for success: Concentration, Discrimination, Organization, Innovation and Communication.**
- Harold S. Geneen 1910 – 1997; American businessman former president of ITT Corporation.

To succeed in your mission, you must have single-minded devotion to your goal.
- Abdul Kalam 1931; Indian scientist, & 11th president of India.

First, have a definite, clear practical ideal; a goal, an objective. Second, have the necessary means to achieve your ends; wisdom, money, materials, and methods. Third, adjust all your means to that end.
- Aristotle 384 BC – 322 BC; Greek philosopher, polymath, & one of the fathers of Western philosophy.

~Success & Failure~

Never give up! Failure and rejection are only the first step to succeeding.
- Jim Valvano 1946 – 1993; American college basketball coach.

All the great things are simple, and many can be expressed in a single word: freedom, justice, honor, duty, mercy, hope.
- Sir Winston Churchill 1874 – 1965; British Prime Minister 1940-1945 & 1951-1955, historian, artist, & Nobel Prize winner in literature.

All that you accomplish or fail to accomplish with your life is the direct result of your thoughts.
- James Allen 1864 – 1912; British writer & poet.

The best way to predict the future is to invent it.
- Alan Kay 1940 –; American computer scientist.

Ability will never catch up with the demand for it.
- Confucius 551 BC – 479 BC; Chinese teacher, politician, & philosopher.

Attack is the best form of defense. (The best defense is a good offense.)
- Dutch Proverb

Optimism is a strategy for making a better future. Because unless you believe that the future can be better, it's unlikely you will step up and take responsibility for making it so. If you assume that there's no hope, you guarantee that there will be no hope. If you assume that there is an instinct for freedom, that there are opportunities to change things, there is a chance you may contribute to making a better world. The choice is yours.
- Noam Chomsky 1928 - ; American linguist, philosopher, cognitive scientist, logician, political commentator, & activist.

Because a thing seems difficult for you, do not think it impossible for anyone to accomplish.
- Marcus Aurelius 121 AD – 180 AD; Roman Emperor, & philosopher.

Play the game for more than you can afford to lose... only then will you learn the game.
- Sir Winston Churchill 1874 – 1965; British Prime Minister 1940-1945 & 1951-1955, historian, artist, & Nobel Prize winner in literature.

It matters not whether you win or lose; what matters is whether I win or lose.
- Darrin Weinberg; Unknown.

Pain is temporary. Quitting lasts forever.
- Lance Armstrong (Lance Edward Gunderson) 1971 - ; American professional cyclist.

Big fish are worth of fishing even if you don't catch one. (When the expectable profits are big enough, risk is worth of taking even if it fails.)
- Finnish Proverb

Being defeated is often only a temporary condition. Giving up is what makes it permanent.
- Marilyn vos Savant 1946 - ; American columnist, author, & lecturer.

Failure is only the opportunity to begin again more intelligently.
- Henry Ford 1863 – 1947; American industrialist, founder of the Ford Motor Company, & developer of the assembly line.

Eighty percent of success is showing up.
- Woody Allen (Allan Stewart Konigsberg) 1935 - ; American comedian, screenwriter, director, actor, author, playwright, musician, & Academy Award winner.

Nothing succeeds like the appearance of success.
- Christopher Lasch 1932 – 1994; American historian, moralist, & social critic.

226

Men get nothing for nothing. (You will get nothing if you do nothing.)
- *Dutch Proverb*

Gold medals aren't really made of gold. They're made of sweat, determination, and a hard-to-find alloy called guts.
- *Dan Gable 1948 - ; American wrestler & head coach.*

It is never too late to be what you might have been.
- *George Eliot (Mary Anne Evans) 1819 – 1880; English novelist.*

The difference between a successful person and others is not lack of strength not a lack of knowledge but rather a lack of will.
- *Vince Lombardi 1913 – 1970; American football player, & coach.*

Create a set of great personal values and surround yourself with the right people that can form your support system. Have an optimistic spirit and develop a strong purpose that you completely believe in and everything you can imagine is possible, for you.
- *Andrew Horton 1962 - ; English business executive.*

You have to expect things of yourself before you can do them.
- *Michael Jordan 1963 - ; American former NBA player, entrepreneur, 6 times NBA champion, & 5 time MVP winner.*

In America, the race goes to the loud, the solemn, the hustler.
- *Gore Vidal 1925 – 2012; American writer, critic, & humorist.*

Some days you're a windshield, some days you're a bug.
- *Price Cobb 1954 - ; American race car driver.*

~Success & Failure~

Only he who does nothing makes no mistakes. (Nothing ventured, nothing gained; He that never climbed, never fell.)
- Russian Proverb

And here is the prime condition of success, the great secret: Concentrate your energy, thought, and capital exclusively upon the business in which you are engaged. Having begun in one line, resolve to fight it out on that line, to lead in it; adopt every improvement, have the best machinery, and know the most about it.
- Andrew Carnegie 1835 – 1919; Scottish American industrialist & philanthropists.

Most people search high and wide for the keys to success. If they only knew, the key to their dreams lies within.
- George Washington Carver 1864 – 1943; American scientist, botanist, educator, & inventor.

I had to make my own living and my own opportunity....Don't sit down and wait for the opportunities to come; you have to get up and make them.
- C.J. Walker (Sarah Breedlove) 1867 – 1919; American entrepreneur & philanthropist. Regarded as the first female self-made millionaire.

I always turn to the sports pages first, which record people's accomplishments. The front page has nothing but man's failures.
- Chief Justice Earl Warren 1891 – 1974; American politician, jurist & governor of California.

Winning isn't everything, but wanting to win is.
- Vince Lombardi 1913 – 1970; American football player, & coach

If a man does not know what port he is steering for, no wind is favorable to him.
- Seneca 4 BC – AD65; Roman philosopher & statesman.

228

~Success & Failure~

Be an individualist and an individual. You'll be amazed at how much faster you get ahead.
- J. Paul Getty 1892 – 1976; American industrialist.

Anytime you see somebody more successful than you are, they are doing something you aren't.
- Malcolm X (Malcolm Little) 1925 – 1965; American human & civil rights activist.

We didn't lose the game; we just ran out of time.
- Vince Lombardi 1913 – 1970; American football player, & coach.

No matter where you go to school, there are many ways to fail and only a few ways to excel.
- Jesse Louis Jackson, Sr. (Jesse Louis Burns) 1941 - ; American civil rights activist & minister.

There are no secrets to success. Don't waste time looking for them. Success is the result of perfection, hard work, learning from failure, loyalty to those for whom you work, and persistence.
- Colin Powell 1937 - ; American retired 4 star general, statesman, & 65th U.S. Secretary Of State.

A diamond is merely a lump of coal that did well under pressure.
- Henry Kissinger (Heinz Alfred Kissinger) 1923 - ; German American statesman, political scientist, U.S. Secretary of State, & Nobel Peace Prize recipient.

Nobody ever wrote down a plan to be broke, fat, lazy, or stupid. Those things are what happen when you don't have a plan.
- Larry Winget 1952 - ; American motivational speaker, author, & TV personality.

A pessimist is one who makes difficulties of opportunities. An optimist makes opportunities of so-called difficulties.
- Sir Winston Churchill 1874 – 1965; British Prime Minister 1940-1945 & 1951-1955, historian, artist, & Nobel Prize winner in literature.

One does not sharpen the axes after the time they are needed.
- Russian Proverb

No one is going to hand me success. I must go out & get it myself. That's why I'm here. To dominate. To conquer. Both the world, and myself.
- Unknown

man or woman accomplishes, but the opposition he or she has to overcome to reach his or her goal.
- Dorothy Height 1912 – 2010; American administrator, educator, civil & woman's rights activist.

A successful man is one who can lay a firm foundation with the bricks others have thrown at him.
- David Brinkley 1920 – 2003; American newscaster.

One of the most important keys to Success is having the discipline to do what you know you should do, even when you don't feel like doing it.
- Unknown

You were not born a winner, and you were not born a loser. You are what you make yourself be.
- Lou Holtz 1937 - ; American football coach, author, & motivational speaker.

Success is the maximum utilization of the ability that you have.
- Zig Ziglar 1926 – 2012; American author & motivational speaker.

230
~Success & Failure~

The temptation to quit will be greatest just before you are about to succeed.
- *Chinese Proverb*

For true success ask yourself these four questions: Why? Why not? Why not me? Why not now?
- *James Allen 1864 – 1912; British writer & poet*

Neither a lofty degree of intelligence nor imagination nor both together go to the making of genius. Love, love, love, that is the soul of genius.
- *Wolfgang Amadeus Mozart (Johannes Chrysostomus Wolfgangus Theophilus Mozart) 1756 – 1791; German influential classical music composer.*

Good timber does not grow with ease; the stronger the wind, the stronger the trees.
- *Willard Marriott 1900 – 1985; American entrepreneur, businessman, & founder of Marriott Hotels.*

Don't let anything stop you. There will be times when you'll be disappointed, but you can't stop.
- *Dr. Sadie T.M. Alexander 1898 – 1989; American lawyer. First African American women to receive a Ph.D. in economics in U.S. & law degree from U. of Pennsylvania Law School.*

There is only one thing that makes a dream impossible to achieve: the fear of failure.
- *Paulo Coelho 1947 - ; Brazilian poet, writer & novelist.*

The height of your accomplishments will equal the depth of your convictions.
- *Unknown*

Perhaps the only limits to the human mind are those we believe in.
- *Willis Harman 1918 – 1997; American engineer, social scientist, academic, futurist, & writer.*

~Success & Failure~

Greatness is not measured by what a
Very close is not home yet. (A miss by an inch is
a miss by a mile.)
- *Haitian Proverb*

They who have conquered doubt and fear have conquered failure.

- *James Allen 1864 – 1912; British writer & poet.*

Champions aren't made in the gyms. Champions are made from something they have deep inside them – a desire, a dream, and a vision. They have to have last-minute stamina, they have to be a little faster, and they have to have the skill and the will. But the will must be stronger than the skill.
- *Muhammad Ali (Cassius Marcellus Clay, Jr.) 1942 - ;*
American Professional Boxing heavyweight champion known
as the greatest boxer of the 20th century.

Success or failure in business is caused more by the mental attitude even than by mental capacities.

- *Walter Scott 1771 – 1832; Scottish playwright, poet, & novelist.*

In the business world today, failure is apparently not an option. We need to change this attitude toward failure - and celebrate the idea that only by falling on our collective business faces do we learn enough to succeed down the road.
- *Naveen Jain 1959 - ; Indian business executive, entrepreneur,*
& philanthropist.

Above all be of single aim; have a legitimate and useful purpose, and devote yourself unreservedly to it.
- *James Allen 1864 – 1912; British writer & poet.*

Don't let slip an opportunity; it may never come again.
- *Chinese Proverb*

Success or failure depends more upon attitude than upon capacity...successful men act as though they have accomplished or are enjoying something. Soon it becomes a reality. Act, look, feel successful, conduct yourself accordingly, and you will be amazed at the positive results.
- *William James 1842 – 1910; American philosopher, psychologist, & physician.*

Mediocrity is now, as formerly, dangerous, commonly fatal, to the poet; but among even the successful writers of prose, those who rise sensibly above it are the very rarest exceptions.
- *William E. Gladstone 1809 – 1898; English politician & 4 time Prime Minister.*

The reason most people never reach their goals is that they don't define them, or ever seriously consider them as believable or achievable. Winners can tell you where they are going, what they plan to do along the way, and who will be sharing the adventure with them.
- *Denis Waitley 1933 - ; American motivational speaker & writer.*

If something is really good, it needs no advertising.
- Hungarian Proverb

Develop success from failures. Discouragement and failure are two of the surest stepping stones to success.
- Dale Carnegie 1888 – 1955; American writer, lecturer, & self-improvement coach.

If a wind blows, ride it!
- Arabic Proverb

~Success & Failure~

~Truth-Consequences-Ethics~

Every man is guilty of all the good he did not do.
- Voltaire (Francois-Marie Arouet) 1694 – 1778; French writer, historian, philosopher, & poet.

Treat those who are good with goodness, and also treat those who are not good with goodness. Thus goodness is attained. Be honest to those who are honest, and be also honest to those who are not honest. Thus honesty is attained.
- Lao Tzu (Laozi) 6th century BC; Ancient Chinese philosopher.

Why should we take advice on sex from the pope? If he knows anything about it, he shouldn't!
- George Bernard Shaw 1856 – 1950; Irish playwright, co-founder of London School of Economics, critic, journalist, Nobel Prize winner, & Oscar winner.

All things are subject to interpretation whichever interpretation prevails at a given time is a function of power and not truth.
- Friedrich Nietzsche 1844 – 1900; German philosopher, philologist, critic, poet, & composer.

Children, fools and drunken men tell the truth. (Children and fools have no inhibition, and alcohol consumed removes the inhibition against telling the truth that occasionally one would like to keep secret.)
- Polish Proverb

Truth is the beginning of every good to the gods, and of every good to man.
- Plato 428 BC – 347 BC; Greek philosopher, mathematician, founder of Academy of Athens (the first institute of higher learning), student of Socrates & teacher of Aristotle.

In law a man is guilty when he violates the rights of others. In ethics he is guilty if he only thinks of doing so.
- Immanuel Kant 1724 – 1804; German philosopher.

Copyright Expired   *Immanuel Kant*

Immanuel Kant 1724 – 1804: German philosopher. *Kant contended that reason is human's source of morality. He tried to bring reason and experience to fill the gaps that philosophy and faith left out. His ideas have influenced history and development of philosophy.*

We have to distrust each other. It is our only defense against betrayal.
- Tennessee Williams (Thomas Lanier Williams III) 1911 – 1983; American Writer, Playwright, 2 time Pulitzer Prize winner, & Poet.

A lie has speed, but truth has endurance.
- Edgar J. Mohn; Unknown.

~Truth-Consequences- Ethics~

Who's talking the truth, does not need a lot of words. (Truth gives a short answer, lies go round about.)
- Polish Proverb

Whenever I hear anyone arguing for slavery, I feel a strong impulse to see it tried on him personally.
- Abraham Lincoln 1809 – 1865; American politician, 16th President of the U.S. during the American Civil war & instrumental in abolishing slavery.

Facts from paper are not the same as facts from people. The reliability of the people giving you the facts is as important as the facts themselves.
- Harold S. Geneen 1910 – 1997; American businessman former president of ITT Corporation.

Honesty is the first chapter in the book of wisdom.
- Thomas Jefferson 1743 – 1826; One of the founding fathers of U.S., the principal author of the Declaration of Independence, & 3rd president of U.S.

Experience is simply the name we give our mistakes.
- Oscar Wilde 1854 – 1900; Irish writer, poet, & playwright.

One is sorry one could not have taken both branches of the road. But we were not allotted multiple selves.
- Gore Vidal 1925 – 2012; American writer, critic, & humorist.

When you are sorrowful look again in your heart, and you shall see that in truth you are weeping for that which has been your delight.
- Khalil Gibran 1883 – 1931; Lebanese artist, poet, & writer.

It is better to die honestly, than to live dishonestly. (Death before dishonor.)
- Latvian Proverb

Anybody can be good in the country. There are no temptations there.
- Oscar Wilde 1854 – 1900; Irish writer, poet, & playwright.

Unswerving loyalty to duty, constant devotion to truth, and a clear conscience will overcome every discouragement and surely lead the way to usefulness and high achievement.
- Grover Cleveland 1837 – 1908; American politician, 22nd and 24th President of the U.S.

Honesty is the best policy.
- Benjamin Franklin 1706 – 1790; American politician, One of the founding fathers of the U.S., polymath, author, postmaster, scientist, musician, inventor, statesmen, critic, & diplomat.

Dancing is a perpendicular expression of a horizontal desire.
- George Bernard Shaw 1856 – 1950; Irish playwright, co-founder of London School of Economics, critic, journalist, Nobel Prize winner, & Oscar winner.

No treaty is ever an impediment to a cheat.
- Sophocles 497 BC – 405 BC; Ancient Greek playwright.

No man has a good enough memory to be a successful liar.
- Abraham Lincoln 1809 – 1865; American politician, 16th President of the U.S. during the American Civil war & instrumental in abolishing slavery.

Good men prefer to be accountable.
- Michael Edwardes 1930 - ; South African business executive.

It is a fine thing to be honest, but it is also very important to be right.
- Sir Winston Churchill 1874 – 1965; British Prime Minister 1940-1945 & 1951-1955, historian, artist, & Nobel Prize winner in literature.

A half-truth is a whole lie.
- English Proverb

If past history was all there was to the game, the richest people would be librarians.
- Warren Buffett 1930 - ; American Business leader, magnate, investor, & philanthropist.

It is best to bite the sour apple. (It is better to confront a harsh reality than to deceive yourself.)
- Swedish Proverb

Speak ill of no man, but speak all the good you know of everybody.
- Benjamin Franklin 1706 – 1790; American politician, One of the founding fathers of the U.S., polymath, author, postmaster, scientist, musician, inventor, statesmen, critic, & diplomat.

The only real failure in life is not to be true to the best one knows.
- Buddha (Gautama Buddha) 563 BCE – 483 BCE; Nepalese (present day) sage that taught principles that Buddhism was founded on.

Better not to exist than live basely (dishonorably).
- Sophocles 497 BC – 405 BC; Ancient Greek playwright.

When a man wants to murder a tiger he calls it sport; when a tiger wants to murder him he calls it ferocity.
- George Bernard Shaw 1856 – 1950; Irish playwright, co-founder of London School of Economics, critic, journalist, Nobel Prize winner, & Oscar winner.

You might as well try to hold an eel by the tail. (Don't take a man by his word)
- Catalan Proverb

Most people who ask for advice from others have already resolved to act as it pleases them.
- Khalil Gibran 1883 – 1931; Lebanese artist, poet, & writer.

The life of man is of no greater importance to the universe than that of an oyster.
- David Hume 1711 – 1776; Scottish skeptic, philosopher, historian, economist, critic, & essayist.

I believe that unarmed truth and unconditional love will have the final word in reality.
- Dr. Martin Luther King, Jr. (Michael King) 1929 - 1968; American clergyman, minister, civil rights activist. Nobel Peace Prize, Presidential Medal of Freedom, & Congressional Gold Medal recipient.

At times of writing I never think what I have said before. My aim is not to be consistent with my previous statements on a given question, but to be consistent with truth as it may present itself to me at a given moment. The result has been that I have grown from truth to truth.
- Mahatma Gandhi (Mohandas Karamchand Gandhi) 1869 – 1948; Indian leader of the Indian nationalism that used non-violent civil disobedience to lead to Indian independence.

Tell the truth and run.
- Yugoslavian Proverb

No lie ever reaches old age.
- Sophocles 497 BC – 405 BC; Ancient Greek playwright.

There are only two mistakes one can make along the road to truth; not going all the way, and not starting.
- Buddha (Gautama Buddha) 563 BCE – 483 BCE; Nepalese (present day) sage that taught principles that Buddhism was founded on.

This report, by its very length, defends itself against the risk of being read.
- Sir Winston Churchill 1874 – 1965; British Prime Minister 1940-1945 & 1951-1955, historian, artist, & Nobel Prize winner in literature.

~Truth-Consequences- Ethics~

Say not, 'I have found the truth,' but rather, 'I have found a truth.'
- Khalil Gibran 1883 – 1931; Lebanese artist, poet, & writer.

The advantage of telling the truth is that nobody ever believes it.
- Dorothy Sayers 1893 – 1957; English crime writer, poet, playwright, & essayist.

If you would be a real seeker after truth, it is necessary that at least once in your life you doubt, as far as possible, all things.
- Rene Descartes (Renatus Cartesius) 1596 – 1650; French philosopher, writer, & mathematician.

Do every act of your life as if it were your last.
- Marcus Aurelius 121 AD – 180 AD; Roman Emperor & philosopher.

Personal example carries more weight than preaching.
- Chinese Proverb

Honest men fear neither the light nor the dark.
- Thomas Fuller 1608 – 1661; English historian & writer.

The worst men often give the best advice.
- Francis Bacon 1561 – 1626; English philosopher, statesman, scientist, orator, & author.

What you don't see with your eyes, don't witness with your mouth.
- English Proverb

The truth should be told, though it kills.
- Timothy Thomas Fortune 1856 – 1928; American civil rights leader and activist, author, journalist, editor, & publisher.

Threats cannot suppress the truth.
- Ida B. Wells-Barnett 1862 – 1931; American journalist, editor, suffragist, sociologist, & civil rights activist.

~Truth-Consequences- Ethics~

Truth gives one reason, the lie gives many. (Truth gives a short answer, lies go round about.)
- *German Proverb*

Nobody speaks the truth when there is something they must have.
- *Elizabeth Bowen 1899 – 1973; Irish novelist.*

Truth is the most valuable thing we have. Let us economize it.
- *Mark Twain (Samuel Langhorne Clemens) 1835-1910; American author & humorist.*

Truth stands, even if there be no public support. It is self-sustained.
- *Mahatma Gandhi (Mohandas Karamchand Gandhi) 1869 – 1948; Indian leader of Indian nationalism that used non-violent civil disobedience to lead to Indian independence.*

Many a true words are spoken in jest.
- *French Proverb*

No enemy is worse than bad advice.
- *Sophocles 497 BC – 405 BC; Ancient Greek playwright.*

There's a lot of humility in the truth and a lot of pride in Ignorance.
- *M.I. Seka 1972 - ; Author & businessman.*

All truths are easy to understand once they are discovered; the point is to discover them.
- *Galileo Galilei 1564 – 1642; Italian physicist, mathematician, astronomer, & philosopher & polymath.*

Cynicism is an unpleasant way of saying the truth.
- *Lillian Hellman 1905 – 1984; American author.*

Truth is certainly a branch of morality and a very important one to society.
- *Thomas Jefferson 1743 – 1826; One of the founding fathers of U.S., the principal author of the Declaration of Independence, & 3rd president of U.S.*

~Truth-Consequences- Ethics~

When in doubt tell the truth.
- Mark Twain (Samuel Langhorne Clemens) 1835-1910; American author & humorist.

Trust arrives walking and departs riding. (To trust someone takes time, but losing someone's trust happens quickly.)
- Dutch Proverb

It isn't true that everyone should follow one path. Listen to your own truth.
- Ram Dass (Richard Alpert) 1931 - ; American spiritual teacher & author.

The language of truth is simple. (Truth gives a short answer, lies go round about.)
- Spanish Proverb

I would rather miss the mark acting well than win the day acting basely (low morals).
- Sophocles 497 BC – 405 BC; Ancient Greek playwright.

~War & Peace~

It is lamentable, that to be a good patriot one must become the enemy of the rest of mankind.
- Voltaire (Francois-Marie Arouet) 1694 – 1778; French writer, historian, philosopher, & poet.

I abhor war and view it as the greatest scourge of mankind.
- Thomas Jefferson 1743 – 1826; One of the founding fathers of U.S., the principal author of the Declaration of Independence, & 3rd president of U.S.

All war is deception.
- Sun Tzu 544 BC – 496 BC; Chinese military general, strategist, & philosopher.

There was never a good war, or a bad peace.
- Benjamin Franklin 1706 – 1790; American politician, One of the founding fathers of the U.S., polymath, author, postmaster, scientist, musician, inventor, statesmen, critic, & diplomat.

World peace, like community peace, does not require that each man love his neighbor -- it requires only that they live together with mutual tolerance, submitting their disputes to a just and peaceful settlement.
- John F. Kennedy 1917-1963; American politician & 35th President of the U.S.

In a battle all you need to make you fight is a little hot blood and the knowledge that it's more dangerous to lose than to win.
- George Bernard Shaw 1856 – 1950; Irish playwright, co-founder of London School of Economics, critic, journalist, Nobel Prize winner, & Oscar winner.

Peace is better than the most just war.
– Latin Proverb

I can make more generals, but horses cost money.
- Abraham Lincoln 1809 – 1865; American politician, 16th President of the U.S. during the American Civil war & instrumental in abolishing slavery.

War is just when it is necessary; arms are permissible when there is no hope except in arms.
- Niccolo Machiavelli 1469 – 1527; Italian historian, politician, diplomat, philosopher, & writer.

You can't say civilization don't advance… in every war they kill you in a new way.
- Will Rogers 1879 – 1935; American humorist, social commentator, actor, & writer.

During war, laws are silent.
– Latin Proverb

If we know that our own men are in a condition to attack, but are unaware that the enemy is not open to attack, we have gone only halfway towards victory.
- Sun Tzu 544 BC – 496 BC; Chinese military general, strategist, & philosopher.

The past is prophetic in that it asserts loudly that wars are poor chisels for carving out peaceful tomorrows.
- Dr. Martin Luther King, Jr. (Michael King) 1929 - 1968; American clergyman, minister, civil rights activist. Nobel Peace Prize, Presidential Medal of Freedom, & Congressional Gold Medal recipient.

Peace is its own reward.
- Mahatma Gandhi (Mohandas Karamchand Gandhi) 1869 – 1948; Indian leader of Indian nationalism that used non-violent civil disobedience to lead to Indian independence.

If there is one principle more deeply rooted in the mind of every American, it is that we should have nothing to do with conquest.
- *Thomas Jefferson 1743 – 1826; One of the founding fathers of U.S., the principal author of the Declaration of Independence, & 3rd president of U.S.*

When envoys are sent with compliments in their mouths, it is a sign that the enemy wishes for a truce.
- *Sun Tzu 544 BC – 496 BC; Chinese military general, strategist, & philosopher.*

Once we have a war there is only one thing to do. It must be won. For defeat brings worse things than any that can ever happen in war.
- *Ernest Hemingway 1899 – 1961; American author, journalist, Pulitzer Prize recipient, & Nobel Prize recipient.*

Nonviolence is a powerful and just weapon....which cuts without wounding and ennobles the man who wields it. It is a sword that heals.
- *Dr. Martin Luther King, Jr. (Michael King) 1929 - 1968; American clergyman, minister, civil rights activist. Nobel Peace Prize, Presidential Medal of Freedom, & Congressional Gold Medal recipient.*

I am a prisoner of hope.
- *Cornel West 1953 - ; American philosopher, academic, activist, author, & professor.*

To the wrongs that need resistance, to the right that needs assistance, to the future in the distance, give yourselves.
- *Carrie Chapman Catt 1859 – 1947; American women's suffrage leader.*

Non-cooperation with evil is as much a duty as is cooperation with good.
- *Mahatma Gandhi (Mohandas Karamchand Gandhi) 1869 – 1948; Indian leader of Indian nationalism that used non-violent civil disobedience to lead to Indian independence.*

246

~War & Peace~

It is from numberless diverse acts of courage and belief that human history is shaped. Each time a man stands up for an ideal, or acts to improve the lot of others, or strikes out against injustice, he sends forth a tiny ripple of hope, and crossing each other from a million different centers of energy and daring, those ripples build a current that can sweep down the mightiest walls of oppression and resistance.
- Robert F. Kennedy 1925-1968; American politician & 64th Us Attorney General.

If fighting is sure to result in victory, than you must fight, even though the ruler forbid it; if fighting will not result in victory, then you must not fight even at the ruler's bidding.
- Sun Tzu 544 BC – 496 BC; Chinese military general, strategist, & philosopher.

Our prime purpose in this life is to help others. And if you can't help them, at least don't hurt them.
- Dalai Lama (spiritual leader of Tibet.) The Dalai Lama is reborn over the centuries into new leaders or teachers. The current one is Tenzin Gyatso born in 1950.

The deepest...dream is not the hunger for money or fame; it is the dream of settling down, in peace and freedom and cooperation.
- Scott Russell Sanders 1945 - ; American novelist & essayist.

Choose love and peace will follow. Choose peace and love will follow.
- Mary Helen Doyle; Unknown.

~War & Peace~

To all those who walk the path of human cooperation war must appear loathsome and inhuman.
- Alfred Adler 1870 – 1937; Austrian physician & psychotherapist.

Men rise from one ambition to another: first, they seek to secure themselves against attack, and then they attack others.
- Niccolo Machiavelli 1469 – 1527; Italian historian, politician, diplomat, philosopher, & writer.

Victorious warriors win first and then go to war, while defeated warriors go to war first and then seek to win.
- Sun Tzu 544 BC – 496 BC; Chinese military general, strategist, & philosopher.

Our loyalties must transcend our race, our tribe, our class, and our nation; and this means we must develop a world perspective.
- Dr. Martin Luther King, Jr. (Michael King) 1929 - 1968; American clergyman, minister, civil rights activist. Nobel Peace Prize, Presidential Medal of Freedom, & Congressional Gold Medal recipient.

War involves in its progress such a train of unforeseen circumstances that no human wisdom can calculate the end; it has but one thing certain, and that is to increase taxes.
- Thomas Paine 1737 – 1809; English-American author, political activist, theorist, & revolutionary.

If civilization is to survive, we must cultivate the science of human relationships - the ability of all peoples, of all kinds, to live together, in the same world at peace.
- Franklin Delano Roosevelt (FDR) 1882 – 1945; American politician, 32nd President of the U.S., & only president to be elected for 4 terms.

The world's people all share the earnest aspiration to have peace, stability, justice and cooperation.
- Tran Duc Luong 1937 - ; Vietnamese president 1997- 2006.

While you are proclaiming peace with your lips, be careful to have it even more fully in your heart.
- St. Francis of Assisi 1181 – 1226; Italian Catholic friar & preacher.

How is it they live in such harmony the billions of stars - when most men can barely go a minute without declaring war in their minds about someone they know.
- Thomas Aquinas 1225 – 1274; Italian friar, priest, philosopher & theologian.

We believe that when men reach beyond this planet, they should leave their national differences behind them.
- John F. Kennedy 1917-1963; American politician & 35th President of the U.S.

He who lives in harmony with himself lives in harmony with the universe.
- Marcus Aurelius 121 AD – 180 AD; Roman Emperor, & philosopher.

All men can see these tactics whereby I conquer, but what none can see is the strategy out of which victory is evolved.
- Sun Tzu 544 BC – 496 BC; Chinese military general, strategist, & philosopher.

It is too difficult to think nobly when one thinks only of earning a living.
- Jean-Jacques Rousseau 1712 – 1778; Swiss French philosopher, writer, & composer.

Invincibility lies in the defense; the possibility of victory in the attack.
- Sun Tzu 544 BC – 496 BC; Chinese military general, strategist, & philosopher.

My attitude to peace is rather based on the Burmese definition of peace - it really means removing all the negative factors that destroy peace in this world. So peace does not mean just putting an end to violence or to war, but to all other factors that threaten peace, such as discrimination, such as inequality, poverty.

- Aung San Suu Kyi 1945 - ; Burmese politician. Nobel Peace Prize, Congressional Gold Medal, & Presidential Medal of Freedom recipient.

He who knows when he can fight and when he cannot, will be victorious.

- Sun Tzu 544 BC – 496 BC; Chinese military general, strategist, & philosopher.

A visitor from Mars could easily pick out the civilized nations. They have the best implements of war.

- Herbert V. Prochnow 1897 – 1998; American banking executive & author.

If you are far from the enemy, make him believe you are near.

- Sun Tzu 544 BC – 496 BC; Chinese military general, strategist, & philosopher.

The opportunity to secure ourselves against defeat lies in our own hands, but the opportunity of defeating the enemy is provided by the enemy himself.

- Sun Tzu 544 BC – 496 BC; Chinese military general, strategist, & philosopher.

~Wealth & Greed~

The man who has won millions at the cost of his conscience is a failure.
- B. C. Forbes 1880 – 1954; Scottish-American financial journalist, author, & founder of Forbes Magazine.

He is rich or poor according to what he is, not according to what he has.
- Henry Ward Beecher 1813-1887; American clergymen, speaker, & abolitionist.

Part of your heritage in this society is the opportunity to become financially independent.
- Jim Rohn 1930 – 2009; American entrepreneur, author, & motivational speaker.

No nation was ever ruined by trade.
- Benjamin Franklin 1706 – 1790; American politician, One of the founding fathers of the U.S., polymath, author, postmaster, scientist, musician, inventor, statesmen, critic, & diplomat.

Out of clutter, find simplicity. From discord, find harmony. In the middle of difficulty lies opportunity.
- Albert Einstein 1879 – 1955; German American theoretical physicist, Nobel Prize winner, & developer of the general theory of relativity.

Deserve, do not ask. (First deserve, then desire.)
- Haitian Proverb.

Lack of money is the root of all evil.
- George Bernard Shaw 1856 – 1950; Irish playwright, co-founder of London School of Economics, critic, journalist, Nobel Prize winner, & Oscar winner.

It is better for you to be free of fear lying upon a pallet, than to have a golden couch and a rich table and be full of trouble.
- Epicurus 341 BC – 270 BC; Greek philosopher.

Honesty is for the most part less profitable than dishonesty.
- Plato 428 BC – 347 BC; Greek philosopher, mathematician, founder of Academy of Athens (the first institute of higher learning), student of Socrates & teacher of Aristotle.

The faults of the burglar are the qualities of the financier.
- George Bernard Shaw 1856 – 1950; Irish playwright, co-founder of London School of Economics, critic, journalist, Nobel Prize winner, & Oscar winner.

The wise man does not lay up his own treasures. The more he gives to others, the more he has for his own.
- Lao Tzu (Laozi) 6th century BC; Ancient Chinese philosopher.

Real riches are the riches possessed inside.
- B. C. Forbes 1880 – 1954; Scottish-American financial journalist, author, & founder of Forbes Magazine.

Of mankind we may say in general they are fickle, hypocritical, and greedy of gain.
- Niccolo Machiavelli 1469 – 1527; Italian historian, politician, diplomat, philosopher, & writer.

The gratification of wealth is not found in mere possession or in lavish expenditure, but in its wise application.
- Miguel de Cervantes (Miguel de Cervantes Saavedra) 1547 – 1616; Spanish novelist, poet, & playwright best known for authoring "Don Quixote".

~Wealth & Greed~

Money, not morality, is the principle commerce of civilized nations.

- Thomas Jefferson 1743 – 1826; One of the founding fathers of U.S., the principal author of the Declaration of Independence, & 3rd president of U.S.

War is the business of barbarians.

- Napoleon Bonaparte 1769 – 1821; French Emperor, military & political leader.

Profit is sweet, even if it comes from deception.

- Sophocles 497 BC – 405 BC; Ancient Greek playwright.

The more money an American accumulates, the less interesting he becomes.

- Gore Vidal 1925 – 2012; American writer, critic, & humorist.

The only wealth which you will keep forever is the wealth you have given away.

Marcus Aurelius 121 AD – 180 AD; Roman Emperor, & philosopher.

Only when the tide goes out do you discover who's been swimming naked.

- Warren Buffett 1930 - ; American Business leader, magnate, investor, & philanthropist.

Prosperity is the best protector of principle.

- Mark Twain (Samuel Langhorne Clemens) 1835-1910; American author & humorist.

There's enough for everyone's need, but not for everyone's greed.

- Mahatma Gandhi (Mohandas Karamchand Gandhi) 1869 – 1948; Indian leader of the Indian nationalism that used non-violent civil disobedience to lead to Indian independence.

Money - like health, love, happiness, and all forms of success that you want to create for yourself - is the result of living purposefully. It is not a goal unto itself.
- Wayne Dyer 1940 - ; American self-help author & motivational speaker.

No one gets rich quickly if he is honest.
- Dutch Proverb.

I am fond of pigs. Dogs look up to us. Cats look down on us. Pigs treat us as equals.
- Sir Winston Churchill 1874 – 1965; British Prime Minister 1940-1945 & 1951-1955, historian, artist, & Nobel Prize winner in literature.

I don't look to jump over 7-foot bars: I look around for 1-foot bars that I can step over.
- Warren Buffett 1930 - ; American Business leader, magnate, investor, & philanthropist.

The lack of money is the root of all evil.
- Mark Twain (Samuel Langhorne Clemens) 1835-1910; American author & humorist.

One today is worth two tomorrows.
- Benjamin Franklin 1706 – 1790; American politician, One of the founding fathers of the U.S., polymath, author, postmaster, scientist, musician, inventor, statesmen, critic, & diplomat.

There are three classes of men; lovers of wisdom, lovers of honor, and lovers of gain.
- Plato 428 BC – 347 BC; Greek philosopher, mathematician, founder of Academy of Athens (the first institute of higher learning), student of Socrates & teacher of Aristotle.

I just need enough money to tide me over until I need more.
- Bill Hoest 1926 – 1988; American cartoonist.

~Wealth & Greed~

It is incumbent on every generation to pay its own debts as it goes. A principle which if acted on would save one-half the wars of the world.
- Thomas Jefferson 1743 – 1826; One of the founding fathers of U.S., the principal author of the Declaration of Independence, & 3rd president of U.S.

The real measure of your wealth is how much you'd be worth if you lost all your money.
- Unknown

Money isn't everything, according to those who have it.
- Malcolm Forbes 1919 – 1990; American publisher of Forbes magazine.

Better a diamond with a flaw than a pebble without.
- Confucius 551 BC – 479 BC; Chinese teacher, politician, & philosopher.

Look at market fluctuations as your friend rather than your enemy; profit from folly rather than participate in it.
- Warren Buffett 1930 - ; American Business leader, magnate, investor, & philanthropist.

In business, words are words; explanations are explanations, promises are promises, but only performance is reality.
- Harold S. Geneen 1910 – 1997; American businessman former president of ITT Corporation.
investor, & philanthropist.

A wise man should have money in his head, but not in his heart.
- Jonathan Swift 1667 – 1745; Irish essayist, satirist, poet, cleric.

Everything costs a lot of money when you haven't got any.
- Joe Louis (Joseph Louis Barrow) 1914 – 1981; American professional boxing champion.

~Wealth & Greed~

Those who have money have in their pockets those who have none.

- Leo Tolstoy (Count Lev Nikolayevich Tolstoy) 1828 – 1910; Russian novelist.

Leo Tolstoy (Count Lev Nikolayevich Tolstoy) 1828 – 1910: Russian novelist. *Regarded as one of the greatest novelists in history for his great novels "War and Peace" and "Anna Karenina". During the 1870's Tolstoy had a spiritual awakening, which followed a literal interpretation of the teachings of Jesus Christ based on the Sermon on the Mount. This caused him to become a fervent pacifist. His beliefs in the teachings of Jesus of turn the other cheek, love they neighbor, and love god had profound impacts on Gandhi and Martin Luther King. He believed the church had perverted the teachings of Christ's and that pacifism and Christianity were one in the same. He also believed that one could find lasting happiness by looking inwards for self-perfection by love than by finding it through guidance of the church or state.*

If you would know the value of money, go and try to borrow some.

- Benjamin Franklin 1706 – 1790; American politician, One of the founding fathers of the U.S., polymath, author, postmaster, scientist, musician, inventor, statesmen, critic, & diplomat.

On Wall Street, enough is never enough.
- Unknown

There was a time when a fool and his money were soon parted, but now it happens to everybody
- Adlai Stevenson IV 1956 - ; American business executive & journalist.

How did a fool and his money get together in the first place?
- Woody Allen (Allan Stewart Konigsberg) 1935 - ; American comedian, screenwriter, director, actor, author, playwright, musician, & Academy Award winner.

It isn't necessary to be rich and famous to be happy. It is only necessary to be rich.
- Alan Alda (Alphonso Joseph D'Abruzzo)1936 – American actor, director, screenwriter, & author.

Gambling is getting nothing for something.
- Wilson Mizner 1876 – 1933; American playwright.

If a man can write a better book, preach a better sermon, or make a better mouse-trap, than his neighbor, though he builds his house in the woods, the world will make a beaten path to his door.
- Ralph Waldo Emerson 1803-1882; American lecturer, poet, & essayist.

The public be damned! I am working for my stock holders.
- William Henry Vanderbilt 1821 – 1885; American businessman.

Corporation, n. An ingenious device for obtaining individual profit without individual responsibility.
- Ambrose Gwinnett Bierce 1824 – 1913; American journalist, writer, & satirist.

Getting and spending, we lay waste our powers.
- William Wordsworth 1770 – 1850; English Romantic poet.

~Wealth & Greed~

Under capitalism, man exploits man. Under communism, it's just the opposite.
- John Kenneth Galbraith 1908 – 2006; Canadian American economist & diplomat.

The Treasury of America depends upon the inventions of unknown men; upon the originations of unknown men, upon the ambitions of unknown men. Every country is renewed out of the ranks of the unknown, not out of the ranks of those already famous and powerful and in control.
- Woodrow Wilson 1856 – 1924; American politician, governor of New Jersey, & 28th President of the U. S.

It's never paid to bet against America. We come through things, but it's not always a smooth ride.
- Warren Buffett 1930 - ; American Business leader, magnate, investor, & philanthropist.

In the US, there is basically one party - the business party. It has two factions, called Democrats and Republicans, which are somewhat different but carry out variations on the same policies. By and large, I am opposed to those policies. As is most of the population.
- Noam Chomsky 1928 - ; American linguist, philosopher, cognitive scientist, logician, political commentator, & activist.

All riches have their origin in mind. Wealth is in ideas - not money.
- Robert Collier 1876 – 1918; American publisher.

Should you find yourself in a chronically leaking boat, energy devoted to changing vessels is likely to be more productive than energy devoted to patching leaks.
- Warren Buffett 1930 - ; American Business leader, magnate, investor, & philanthropist.

~Wealth & Greed~

**2 things a good businessman must do;
Increase revenue and reduce costs.
Every decision must be made around
these 2 principles.**
- M.I. Seka 1972 - ; Author & businessman.

**If you deprive yourself of outsourcing
and your competitors do not, you're
putting yourself out of business.**
*- Lee Kuan Yew 1923 - ; Singaporean politician & Prime
Minister for 3 decades.*

**When a management with a reputation
for brilliance tackles a business with a
reputation for bad economics, it is the
reputation of the business that remains
intact.**
- Warren Buffett 1930 - ; American Business leader, magnate,

The work of the individual still remains the spark that moves mankind ahead even more than teamwork.
*- Igor Sikorsky 1889 – 1972; Russian American aviation
pioneer.*

**In the social business marketplace,
brands that hope to build loyal and
growing communities do so most
effectively when they demonstrate their
core values and allow a community to
build and engage around it.**
- Simon Mainwaring 1967 - ; Australian business consultant.

**One thing is certain in business. You and
everyone around you will make
mistakes.**
- Richard Branson 1950 - ; English businessman & investor.

**A business like an automobile has to be
driven, in order to get results.**
*- B. C. Forbes 1880 – 1954; Scottish-American financial
journalist, author, & founder of Forbes Magazine.*

The entrepreneur always searches for change, responds to it, and exploits it as an opportunity.

- Peter F. Drucker 1909 – 2005; Austrian American educator & author.

Business is the salt of life.

- Voltaire (Francois-Marie Arouet) 1694 – 1778; French writer, historian, philosopher, & poet.

America doesn't respect anything but money.

- C.J. Walker (Sarah Breedlove) 1867 – 1919; American entrepreneur & philanthropist. Regarded as the first female self-made millionaire.

Capital isn't that important in business. Experience isn't that important. You can get both of these things. What is important is ideas.

- Harvey S. Firestone 1868 – 1938; American businessman.

I am just absolutely convinced that the best formula for giving us peace and preserving the American way of life is freedom, limited government, and minding our own business overseas.

- Ron Paul 1935 - ; American politician, physician, & author.

In this business, by the time you realize you're in trouble, it's too late to save yourself. Unless you're running scared all the time, you're gone.

- Bill gates (William Henry Gates III) 1955 - ; American business magnate, investor, programmer, inventor, co-founder of Microsoft, & philanthropist.

I think the most important factor in getting out of the recession actually is just the regenerative capacity of - of American capitalism.

- Warren Buffett 1930 - ; American Business leader, magnate, investor, & philanthropist.

~Wealth & Greed~

Labour was the first price, the original purchase - money that was paid for all things. It was not by gold or by silver, but by labour, that all wealth of the world was originally purchased.

- Adam Smith 1723 – 1790; Scottish philosopher, pioneer of economic theory, & author of "The inquiry into the nature and causes of the Wealth of Nations" in 1776 or better known as "Wealth of Nations".

~Words of Wisdom & Enlightenment~

Each player must accept the cards life deals him or her: but once they are in hand, he or she alone must decide how to play the cards in order to win the game.
- Voltaire (Francois-Marie Arouet) 1694 – 1778; French writer, historian, philosopher, & poet.

He who has a why to live can bear almost any how.
- Friedrich Nietzsche 1844 – 1900; German philosopher, philologist, critic, poet, & composer.

He that lives upon hope will die fasting.
- Benjamin Franklin 1706 – 1790; American politician, One of the founding fathers of the U.S., polymath, author, postmaster, scientist, musician, inventor, statesmen, critic, & diplomat.

There are only two tragedies in life: one is not getting what one wants, and the other is getting it.
- Oscar Wilde 1854 – 1900; Irish writer, poet, & playwright.

Justice... is a kind of compact not to harm or be harmed.
- Epicurus 341 BC – 270 BC; Greek philosopher.

Whenever you do a thing, act as if all the world were watching.
- Thomas Jefferson 1743 – 1826; One of the founding fathers of U.S., the principal author of the Declaration of Independence, & 3rd president of U.S.

Opportunities multiply as they are seized.

- Sun Tzu 544 BC – 496 BC; Chinese military general, strategist, & philosopher.

Sun Tzu 544 BC – 496 BC: Chinese military general, strategist, & philosopher. *Known for this book "The Art of War" on military strategy, Sun Tzu was also a legendary historic figure in Chinese history and culture. Some controversy remain as to the true authenticity of authorship since his descendant Sun Bin also known as Sun Tzu, also wrote on military tactics titled "The Art of War". The book presents the philosophy of war as well as managing conflicts and winning battles and/or wars. The Art of War has been and continues to be used by politicians, generals, businessmen, and highly ambitious people.*

Success is almost totally dependent upon drive and persistence. The extra energy required to make another effort or try another approach is the secret of winning.

- Denis Waitley 1933 - ; American writer, author, & motivational speaker.

Enjoy the little things, for one day you may look back and realize they were the big things.

- Robet Brault; Writer.

Wisdom outweighs any wealth.

- Sophocles 497 BC – 405 BC; Ancient Greek playwright.

In dwelling, live close to the ground. In thinking, keep to the simple. In conflict, be fair and generous. In governing, don't try to control. In work, do what you enjoy. In family life, be completely present.
- Lao Tzu (Laozi) 6th century BC; Ancient Chinese philosopher.

Virtue consists, not in abstaining from vice, but in not desiring it.
- George Bernard Shaw 1856 – 1950; Irish playwright, co-founder of London School of Economics, critic, journalist, Nobel Prize winner, & Oscar winner.

Things may come to those who wait, but only the things left by those who hustle.
- Abraham Lincoln 1809 – 1865; American politician, 16th President of the U.S. during the American Civil war & instrumental in abolishing slavery.

All the gold which is under or upon the earth is not enough to give in exchange for virtue (moral excellence, goodness).
- Plato 428 BC – 347 BC; Greek philosopher, mathematician, founder of Academy of Athens (the first institute of higher learning), student of Socrates & teacher of Aristotle.

The best way to predict the future is to create it.
- Peter Drucker 1909 – 2005; American businessman.

Knowledge of the self is the mother of all knowledge. So it is incumbent on me to know myself, to know it completely, to know its minutiae, its characteristics, its subtleties, and its very atoms.
- Khalil Gibran 1883 – 1931; Lebanese artist, poet, & writer.

A person who never made a mistake never tried anything new.
- Albert Einstein 1879 – 1955; German American theoretical physicist, Nobel Prize winner, & developer of the general theory of relativity.

In youth and beauty, wisdom is but rare!

- Homer 7th or 8th century BC; Ancient Greek author of the Iliad and the Odyssey, poet, & orator.

Homer 7th or 8th century BC: Ancient Greek author of the *Iliad* and *The Odyssey*, Poet, & orator. *Thought of as one of the greatest ancient Greek poets, whose works continue to have significance prominence on Western literature.*

The wise stand out because they see themselves as part of the Whole. They shine because they don't want to impress. They achieve great things because they don't look for recognition. Their wisdom is contained in what they are, not their opinions. They refuse to argue, so no-one argues with them.
- Lao Tzu (Laozi) 6th century BC; Ancient Chinese philosopher.

We must all suffer one of two things: the pain of discipline or the pain of regret or disappointment.

- Jim Rohn 1930 – 2009; American entrepreneur, author, & motivational speaker.

~Words of Wisdom & Enlightenment~

The surest way to corrupt a youth is to instruct him to hold in higher esteem those who think alike than those who think differently.
- Friedrich Nietzsche 1844 – 1900; German philosopher, philologist, critic, poet, & composer.

The difficulties you meet will resolve themselves as you advance. Proceed, and light will dawn, and shine with increasing clearness on your path.
- Jim Rohn 1930 – 2009; American entrepreneur, author, & motivational speaker.

Any fool can criticize, condemn and complain - and most fools do.
- Benjamin Franklin 1706 – 1790; American politician, One of the founding fathers of the U.S., polymath, author, postmaster, scientist, musician, inventor, statesmen, critic, & diplomat.

Of soup and love the first is the best.
- Lithuanian Proverb

Courage is the first of human qualities because it is the quality which guarantees the others.
- Aristotle 384 BC – 322 BC; Greek philosopher, polymath, & one of the fathers of Western philosophy.

If God did not exist, it would be necessary to invent Him.
- Voltaire (Francois-Marie Arouet) 1694 – 1778; French writer, historian, philosopher, & poet.

The young do not know enough to be prudent, and therefore they attempt the impossible -- and achieve it, generation after generation.
- Pearl S. Buck 1892 – 1973; American writer, novelist, Pulitzer Prize recipient, & Nobel Prize in Literature recipient.

Wisdom outweighs any wealth.
- Sophocles 497 BC – 405 BC; Ancient Greek playwright.

~Words of Wisdom & Enlightenment~

We should not permit our grievances to overshadow our opportunities.

- Booker T. (Taliaferro) Washington 1856 – 1915; American educator, orator, author, & advisor to the Presidents of the United States.

Booker T. (Taliaferro) Washington 1856 – 1915: African American educator, orator, author, & advisor to the Presidents of the United States. *Born into slavery, he worked his way to becoming a leading voice of former slaves facing new oppressive environment of discrimination, Jim Crow Laws, and disfranchisement by the Southern states. He called for the Atlanta compromise to avoid confrontation with Southern whites. As lynching was reaching a peak, he didn't want to exasperate the problem by publically challenging Jim Crow laws or black voting suppression laws. He advocated long-term goals of community economic strength, pride, self-help, and education.*

Where the willingness is great, the difficulties cannot be great.

- Niccolo Machiavelli 1469 – 1527; Italian historian, politician, diplomat, philosopher, & writer.

In the midst of great joy, do not promise anyone anything. In the midst of great anger, do not answer anyone's letter.

- Chinese proverb

When dealing with people, remember you are not dealing with creatures of logic, but creatures of emotion.
- Dale Carnegie 1888 – 1955; American writer, lecturer, & self-improvement coach.

Wisdom alone is the science of other sciences.
- Plato 428 BC – 347 BC; Greek philosopher, mathematician, founder of Academy of Athens (the first institute of higher learning), student of Socrates & teacher of Aristotle.

Always bear in mind that your own resolution to succeed is more important than any other.
- Abraham Lincoln 1809 – 1865; American politician, 16th President of the U.S. during the American Civil war & instrumental in abolishing slavery.

Do all the good you can, by all the means you can, in all the ways you can, in all the places you can, to all the people you can, as long as you ever can.
- John Wesley 1703 – 1791; English Anglican cleric & theologian.

Religion is something left over from the infancy of our intelligence, it will fade away as we adopt reason and science as our guidelines.
- Bertrand Russell 1872 – 1970; English philosopher, logician, mathematician, historian, critic, & Nobel Prize in Literature recipient.

When anger rises, think of the consequences.
- Confucius 551 BC – 479 BC; Chinese teacher, politician, & philosopher.

There exists no rule without exceptions.
(There is no rule without an exception.)
- Dutch Proverb

~Words of Wisdom & Enlightenment~

Old age and the passage of time teach all things.
- *Sophocles 497 BC – 405 BC; Ancient Greek playwright.*

Age wrinkles the body. Quitting wrinkles the soul.
- *Douglas MacArthur 1880 – 1964; American general & Medal of Honor winner.*

If you don't help yourself, even God cannot help you.
- *Bulgarian Proverb*

The teacher who is indeed wise does not bid you to enter the house of his wisdom but rather leads you to the threshold of your mind.
- *Khalil Gibran 1883 – 1931; Lebanese artist, poet, & writer.*

To the mind that is still, the whole universe surrenders.
- *Lao Tzu (Laozi) 6th century BC; Ancient Chinese philosopher.*

One sleeps like one makes his bed. (Actions have consequences.)
- *Finnish Proverb*

I am somebody!
- *Jesse Louis Jackson, Sr. (Jesse Louis Burns) 1941 - ; American civil rights activist & minister.*

Remember the things in life that are free to each of us—our family, our friends, our soul, our hopes, our dreams, and our knowledge—are the most important.
- *Jaren L. Davis; Unknown.*

A word to the wise ain't necessary. It's the stupid who need the advice.
- *Bill Cosby 1937 - ; American comedian, actor, author, & educator.*

Skip the enjoyment that you will regret.
(Avoid the pleasure which will bite tomorrow.)
- *Italian Proverb*

269

~Words of Wisdom & Enlightenment~

To refrain from imitation is the best revenge.

- Marcus Aurelius 121 AD – 180 AD; Roman Emperor, & philosopher.

Marcus Aurelius 121 AD – 180 AD: Roman Emperor & philosopher. *Was one of the last great emperors of Rome. Marcus Aurelius was known as a philosopher king. Between 170 AD and 180 AD, he wrote a diary titled "To Myself", which had rules for guidance and self-improvement. The work was published after his death and retitled "Meditations".*

The highest form of spiritual work is the realization of the essence of man.... You never learn the answer; you can only become the answer.

- Richard Rose; Unknown.

Wisdom comes alone through suffering.

- Aeschylus 525 BC – 455 BC; Ancient Greek tragic playwright.

If you think in terms of a year, plant a seed; if in terms of ten years, plant trees; if in terms of 100 years, teach the people.

- Confucius 551 BC – 479 BC; Chinese teacher, politician, & philosopher.

The man who is intent on making the most of his opportunities is too busy to bother about luck.
- B. C. Forbes 1880 – 1954; Scottish-American financial journalist, author, & founder of Forbes Magazine.

The more man meditates upon good thoughts; the better will be his world and the world at large.
- Confucius 551 BC – 479 BC; Chinese teacher, politician, & philosopher.

Whatever is begun in anger ends in shame.
- Benjamin Franklin 1706 – 1790; American politician, One of the founding fathers of the U.S., polymath, author, postmaster, scientist, musician, inventor, statesmen, critic, & diplomat.

Optimism is the faith that leads to achievement. Nothing can be done without hope and confidence.
- Helen Adams Keller 1880 – 1968; American author, political activist, first deaf blind person to earn a B.A. & lecturer.

Life isn't about finding yourself. Life is about creating yourself.
- George Bernard Shaw 1856 – 1950; Irish playwright, co-founder of London School of Economics, critic, journalist, Nobel Prize winner, & Oscar winner.

Walk with the dreamers, the believers, the courageous, the cheerful, the planners, the doers, the successful people with their heads in the clouds and their feet on the ground. Let their spirit ignite a fire within you to leave this world better than when you found it.
- Wilferd A. Peterson 1900 – 1995; American author.

~Words of Wisdom & Enlightenment~

Everything is a gift of the universe - even joy, anger, jealously, frustration, or separateness. Everything is perfect either for our growth or our enjoyment.
- *Ken Keyes Jr. 1921 – 1995; Author & lecturer.*

Wisdom alone is true ambition's aim; wisdom is the source of virtue and of fame; obtained with labor, for mankind employed, and then, when most you share it, best enjoyed.
- *Alfred North Whitehead 1861 – 1947; English philosopher & mathematician.*

Sorrow is knowledge, those that know the most must mourn the deepest, the tree of knowledge is not the tree of life.
- *Lord Byron (George Gordon Byron) 1788 – 1824; English poet & writer.*

A candle loses nothing by lighting another candle. (You don't lose anything by enlightening others.)
- *English Proverb*

Buy land, they're not making it anymore.
- *Mark Twain (Samuel Langhorne Clemens) 1835-1910; American author & humorist.*

Without a sense of urgency, desire loses its value.
- *Jim Rohn 1930 – 2009; American entrepreneur, author, & motivational speaker.*

Suffering is but another name for the teaching of experience, which is the parent of instruction and the schoolmaster of life.
- *Horace 65 BC – 8 BC; Roman poet.*

Admiration is the daughter of ignorance. (People often admire others about whom they only have incomplete knowledge.)
- *English Proverb*

~Words of Wisdom & Enlightenment~

Herein lies the tragedy of the age; not that men are poor....not that men are wicked....but that men know so little of men.

- W.E.B. (William Edward Burghardt) Du Bois 1868 – 1963; American sociologist, historian, civil rights activist, author, professor, co-founder of the NAACP & editor.

W.E.B. (William Edward Burghardt) Du Bois 1868 – 1963: American sociologist, historian, civil rights activist, author, professor, & co-founder of the NAACP & editor. *The first African American to earn a doctorate from Harvard, Du Bois became the leader of the Niagara Movement that worked for equal rights for blacks. Du Bois opposed the Atlanta Compromise brought forth by Booker T. Washington that wanted to negotiate with southern whites that called for blacks to submit to white political rule in exchange for basic education and limited economic opportunities. Du Bois wanted full civil rights and political representation. Many of the reforms he fought for his entire life was enacted in the Civil Rights Act a year after his death.*

He who wants the heavens must pay. (If you want the best, you have to work for it or, it will cost you).
- Spanish Proverb

Motivation is what gets you started. Habit is what keeps you going.
- Jim Ryun 1947 - ; American politician & athlete.

~Words of Wisdom & Enlightenment~

How do we nurture the soul? By revering our own life. By learning to love it all, not only the joys and the victories, but also the pain and the struggles.

- Nathaniel Branden (Nathan Blumenthal) 1930 - ; Canadian psychotherapist & writer.

To lengthen thy life, lessen thy meals.

- Benjamin Franklin 1706 – 1790; American politician, One of the founding fathers of the U.S., polymath, author, postmaster, scientist, musician, inventor, statesmen, critic, & diplomat.

Opinions have greater power than strength of hands.

- Sophocles 497 BC – 405 BC; Ancient Greek playwright.

Attitude is a little thing that makes a big difference.

- Sir Winston Churchill 1874 – 1965; British Prime Minister 1940-1945 & 1951-1955, historian, artist, & Nobel Prize winner in literature.

If you can find a path with no obstacles, it probably doesn't lead anywhere.

- Frank Clark 1860 – 1936; American politician.

Common sense in an uncommon degree is what the world calls wisdom.

- Samuel Taylor Coleridge 1772 – 1834; English poet, literary critic, & philosopher.

Whatever nature has in store for mankind, unpleasant as it may be, men must accept, for ignorance is never better than knowledge.

- Enrico Fermi 1901 – 1954; Italian physicist, one of the "fathers of the atomic bomb", & Nobel Prize recipient in physics.

A good deed never goes unpunished.
- Gore Vidal 1925 – 2012; American writer, critic, & humorist.

True knowledge exists in knowing that you know nothing.
- Socrates 469 BC – 399BC; Ancient Greek philosopher.

Beware the man of one book. (A man who reads only the same type of books is indirectly dangerous to himself and others because of his ignorance.)
- Latin Proverb

He who knows other is learned; he who knows himself is wise.
- Lao Tzu (Laozi) 6th century BC; Ancient Chinese philosopher.

A man may die, nations may rise and fall, but an idea lives on.
- John F. Kennedy 1917-1963; American politician & 35th President of the U.S.

A man begins cutting his wisdom teeth the first time he bites off more than he can chew.
- Herb Caen 1916 – 1997; American journalist, satirist, critic & Pulitzer Prize winner.

Go ahead and do it. It's much easier to apologize after something's been done than to get permission ahead of time.
- Grace Hopper 1906 – 1992; American computer scientist.

The man of knowledge must be able not only to love his enemies but also to hate his friends.
- Friedrich Nietzsche 1844 – 1900; German philosopher, philologist, critic, poet, & composer.

You cannot belong to anyone else until you belong to yourself.
- Pearl Bailey 1918 – 1990; American actress, singer, & Tony Award winner.

~Words of Wisdom & Enlightenment~

None is nobler in life than to be a Creator.
- M.I. Seka – 1972 - ; Author & businessman.

About morals, I know only that what is moral is what you feel good after and what is immoral is what you feel bad after.
- Ernest Hemingway 1899 – 1961; American author, journalist, Pulitzer Prize recipient, & Nobel Prize recipient.

Ernest Hemingway 1899 – 1961; American author & journalist. *More than an author, Hemingway led a life full of adventure, which influenced future generations for decades to come. After high school, Hemingway enlisted as an ambulance driver in WWI. After being seriously wounded, he returned home to Illinois. In 1927, he returned to Europe as a journalist to cover the Spanish Civil War. Hemingway spent most of his travels abroad in various journalistic positions. He was also present at the Normandy Landings in WWII. Hemingway had a home in Key West, Florida and another in Cuba. He won the Pulitzer Prize for Fiction and the Nobel Prize in Literature. Many of his works are considered classics of American literature.*

Death is nothing, but to live defeated and inglorious is to die daily.
- Napoleon Bonaparte 1769 – 1821; French Emperor, military & political leader.

Self-suggestion makes you master of yourself.
- W. Clement Stone 1902 – 2002; American self-help author, businessman, & philanthropist.

~Words of Wisdom & Enlightenment~

I was always looking outside myself for strength and confidence but it comes from within. It is there all the time.
- Anna Freud 1895 – 1982; Austrian psychoanalyst, daughter of Sigmund Freud, & founder of psychoanalytic child psychology.

Walking in space, man has never looked more puny or more significant.
- Alexander Chase 1926 - ; American journalist.

The man who never makes a mistake gets tired of doing nothing.
- Will Rogers 1879 – 1935; American humorist, social commentator, actor, & writer.

The genius, wit, and the spirit of a nation are discovered by their proverbs.
- Francis Bacon 1561 – 1626; English philosopher, statesman, scientist, orator, & author.

As you walk down the fairway of life you must smell the roses, for you only get to play one round.
- Ben Hogan 1912 – 1997; American professional golfer.

From the errors of others, a wise man corrects his own.
- Publilius Syrus 1st century BC; Syrian former slave, writer, & playwright.

Experience is a hard teacher because she gives the test first, the lesson afterwards.
- Vernon Sanders Law 1930 - ; American baseball pitcher.

Experience keeps a dear school. (Wisdom acquired by experience is basically only very bitterly acquired.)
- Spanish Proverb

The realization of ignorance is the first act of knowing.
- Jean Toomer 1894 – 1967; American author & poet.

All my limitations are self-imposed, and my liberation can only come from true self-love.
- Max Robinson 1939 – 1988; American broadcast journalist, & civil rights activist.

Nothing is more powerful and liberating than knowledge.
- William H. Gray III 1941 – 2013; American politician.

A genuine leader is not a searcher for consensus but a molder of consensus.
- Dr. Martin Luther King, Jr. (Michael King) 1929 - 1968; American clergyman, minister, civil rights activist. Nobel Peace Prize, Presidential Medal of Freedom, & Congressional Gold Medal recipient.

It doesn't have to glitter to be gold.
- Arthur Ashe (Arthur Robert Ashe, Jr. 1943 – 1993; American top professional Tennis player & Presidential Medal of Freedom recipient.

The less you talk, the more you're listened to.
- Abigail Van Buren (Pauline Esther Phillips) AKA "Dear Abby" 1918 – 2013; American advice columnist & radio show host.

It's when you're down that you learn about your faults.
- Claude McKay 1889 – 1948; Jamaican American writer & poet.

Nature and books belong to the eyes that see them.
- Ralph Waldo Emerson 1803-1882; American lecturer, poet, & essayist.

Winning is not everything, but wanting to win is.
- Vince Lombardi 1913 – 1970; American football player, & coach.

Some days you get the bear, other days the bear gets you. (You can't always expect only positive results.)
- English Proverb

90% of everything is crap.
- Theodore Sturgeon (Edward Hamilton Waldo) 1918 – 1985; American writer & critic.

Be secret and exult (highly joyous), Because of all things known that is most difficult.
- William Butler Yeats 1865 – 1939; Irish poet, politician, & Nobel Prize in Literature recipient.

A fool flatters himself; a wise man flatters the fool.
- Edward G. Bulwer-Lytton 1803 – 1873; English novelist, poet, playwright, & politician.

Honesty is the best policy.
- Benjamin Franklin 1706 – 1790; American politician, One of the founding fathers of the U.S., polymath, author, postmaster, scientist, musician, inventor, statesmen, critic, & diplomat.

The truth is not for all men, but only for those who seek it.
- Ayn Rand (Alisa Zinov'yevna Rosenbaum) 1905 – 1982; Russian-American novelist, playwright, & screenwriter.

There is a wisdom of the head, and a wisdom of the heart.
- Charles Dickens 1812 – 1870; English writer & critic.

Wisdom is found only in truth.
– Johann Wolfang Von Goethe 1749 – 1832; German writer & politician.

To be satisfied with a little, is the greatest wisdom; and he that increaseth his riches, increaseth his cares; but a contented mind is a hidden treasure, and trouble findeth it not.
- Akhenaten ? – 1334 BC; Ancient Egyptian Pharaoh.

Patience is the companion of wisdom.
- Saint Augustine (Augustine of Hippo) 354 – 430; Ancient Roman theologian, author, philosopher, & developed the idea of the central Catholic Church & original sin.

The young man knows the rules, but the old man knows the exceptions.
- Oliver Wendell Holmes, Sr. 1809 - 1894; American physician, poet, professor, lecturer, author.

To conquer fear is the beginning of wisdom.
- Bertrand Russell 1872 – 1970; English philosopher, logician, mathematician, historian, critic, & Nobel Prize in Literature recipient.

Without suffering, there is no learning. (No pain, no gain; Nothing ventured, nothing gained.)
- Croatian Proverb

It is the nature of the wise to resist pleasures, but the foolish to be a slave to them.
- Epictetus 55-135; Ancient Greek sage & philosopher.

Man is only great when he acts from passion.
- Benjamin Disraeli 1804 – 1881; English politician, writer, & 2 time Prime Minister.

Knowledge is of no value unless you put it into practice.
- Anton Chekhov 1860 – 1904; Russian physician & author.

No man was ever wise by chance.
- Seneca 4 BC – AD65; Roman philosopher & statesman.

Better be wise by the misfortunes of others than by your own.
- Aesop 620 BC – 564 BC; Ancient Greek story teller.

The truest wisdom is a resolute determination.
- Napoleon Bonaparte 1769 – 1821; French Emperor, military & political leader.

Always seek out the seed of triumph in every adversity.
- Augustine "Og" Mandino II 1923 – 1996; American author.

~Words of Wisdom & Enlightenment~

Honesty is the rarest wealth anyone can possess, and yet all the honesty in the world ain't lawful tender for a loaf of bread.
- Josh Billings (Henry Wheeler Shaw) 1818 – 1885; American humorist, writer, & lecturer.

Knowledge comes, but wisdom lingers.
- Alfred Lord Tennyson 1809 – 1892; English poet.

Wisdom outweighs any wealth.
- Sophocles 497 BC – 405 BC; Ancient Greek playwright.

The more intense the nature of a man, the more readily will he find meditation, and the more successfully will he practice it.
- James Allen 1864 – 1912; British writer & poet.

Those who improve with age embrace the power of personal growth and personal achievement and begin to replace youth with wisdom, innocence with understanding, and lack of purpose with self-actualization.
- Bo Bennett 1972 - ; American businessman & author.

To keep your secret is wisdom; but to expect others to keep it is folly.
- Samuel Johnson 1709 – 1784; English writer, poet, essayist, critic, editor, & author of the first English dictionary.

War involves in its progress such a train of unforeseen circumstances that no human wisdom can calculate the end; it has but one thing certain, and that is to increase taxes.
- Thomas Paine 1737 – 1809; English-American author, political activist, theorist, & revolutionary.

A proverb is the wisdom of many and the wit of one.
- Lord John Russell 1792 – 1878; English politician and 2 time Prime minister of the U.K.

Teach this triple truth to all: A generous heart, kind speech, and a life of service and compassion are the things that renew humanity.

- Buddha (Gautama Buddha) 563 BCE – 483 BCE; Nepalese (present day) sage that taught principles that Buddhism was founded on.

Buddha (Gautama Buddha) 563 BCE – 483 BCE; Nepalese (present day) sage that taught principles that Buddhism was founded on. *With a name meaning "awakened one" or "enlightened one", Buddha was believed to have been born of a virgin with super natural abilities, such as having no need for sleep, food, or medicine, as well as the ability to control life energy or "Karma". Born into nobility, Buddha left his lavish lifestyle at age 29 in search of enlightenment. After nearly dying of self-inflicted starvation, Buddha vowed that he would meditate until he attained enlightenment. After 49 days of meditation, he is said to have attained enlightenment and was from then on known as Buddha. Buddha claimed insight into the causes of suffering and knew ways to eliminate them. These discoveries became known as the "Four Noble Truths." Mastering these truths will help to achieve Nirvana or enlightenment. At the age of 80, Buddha announced that he would be leaving his earthly body. After eating his last meal, he fell ill, asked his followers if they had any further questions or doubts (which they did not), and died shortly after. His final words were "all composite things are perishable. Strive for your own liberation with diligence."*

Follow your own star!

- Dante Alighieri 1265 – 1321; Italian poet & author of "Divine Comedy".

282

Knowledge can be communicated, but not wisdom. One can find it, live it, be fortified by it, do wonders through it, but one cannot communicate and teach it.
- Hermann Hesse 1877 – 1962; German Swill poet, novelist, painter & Nobel Prize winner in Literature.

All men by nature desire knowledge.
- Aristotle 384 BC – 322 BC; Greek philosopher, polymath, & one of the fathers of Western philosophy.

Mainstream media tend to just mouth the conventional wisdom, to see everything through the filter of right and left.
- Arianna Huffington 1950 - ; Greek American author & syndicated columnist.

Knowledge which is divorced from justice may be called cunning rather than wisdom.
- Marcus Tullius Cicero 106 BC – 43BC; Roman philosopher, politician, lawyer, orator, political theorist, consul, & constitutionalist.

The wisdom of the wise and the experience of the ages are preserved into perpetuity by a nation's proverbs, fables, folk sayings and quotations.
- William Feather 1889 – 1981; American publisher & author.

The only medicine for suffering, crime, and all other woes of mankind, is wisdom. Teach a man to read and write, and you have put into his hands the great keys of the wisdom box. But it is quite another thing to open the box.
- Thomas Henry Huxley 1825 – 1895; English biologist.

A wise man does not chatter with one whose mind is sick.
- Sophocles 497 BC – 405 BC; Ancient Greek playwright.

~Work & Action~

It is the working man who is the happy man. It is the idle man who is the miserable man.
- Benjamin Franklin 1706 – 1790; American politician, One of the founding fathers of the U.S., polymath, author, postmaster, scientist, musician, inventor, statesmen, critic, & diplomat.

The secret of being miserable is to have leisure to bother about whether you are happy or not. The cure for it is occupation.
- George Bernard Shaw 1856 – 1950; Irish playwright, co-founder of London School of Economics, critic, journalist, Nobel Prize winner, & Oscar winner.

Of all that is written, I love only what a person has written with his own blood.
- Friedrich Nietzsche 1844 – 1900; German philosopher, philologist, critic, poet, & composer.

Do you want to know who you are? Don't ask. Act! Action will delineate and define you.
- Thomas Jefferson 1743 – 1826; One of the founding fathers of U.S., the principal author of the Declaration of Independence, & 3rd president of U.S.

To be idle is a short road to death and to be diligent is a way of life; foolish people are idle, wise people are diligent.
- Buddha (Gautama Buddha) 563 BCE – 483 BCE; Nepalese (present day) sage that taught principles that Buddhism was founded on.

Success is dependent on effort.
- Sophocles 497 BC – 405 BC; Ancient Greek playwright.

Adversity has the effect of eliciting talents, which in prosperous circumstances would have lain dormant.

- Horace 65 BC – 8 BC; Roman poet.

Horace (Quintus Horatius Flaccus) 65 BC – 8 BC; Roman poet. *A major Latin Lyric poet during the Augustan age. He is best known today for poet's commemorating common things like toasting a drink or well wishing in very simplistic, precise, & easily expressive words.*

When you are laboring for others let it be with the same zeal as if it were for yourself.

- Confucius 551 BC – 479 BC; Chinese teacher, politician, & philosopher.

Never confuse movement with action.

- Ernest Hemingway 1899 – 1961; American author, journalist, Pulitzer Prize recipient, & Nobel Prize recipient.

Walk the walk and talk the talk. (First do your task, and then talk about it.)
- English Proverb

Performance stands out like a ton of diamonds. Nonperformance can always be explained away.
- Harold S. Geneen 1910 – 1997; American businessman former president of ITT Corporation.

Success is not the key to happiness. Happiness is the key to success. If you love what you are doing, you will be successful.
- Herman Cain 1945 - ; American business executive, author, radio host & columnist.

You can discover more about a person in an hour of play than in a year of conversation.
- Plato 428 BC – 347 BC; Greek philosopher, mathematician, founder of Academy of Athens (the first institute of higher learning), student of Socrates & teacher of Aristotle.

I have nothing to offer but blood, toil, tears and sweat.
- Sir Winston Churchill 1874 – 1965; British Prime Minister 1940-1945 & 1951-1955, historian, artist, & Nobel Prize winner in literature.

The major reason for setting a goal is for what it makes of you to accomplish it. What it makes of you will always be the far greater value than what you get.
- Jim Rohn 1930 – 2009; American entrepreneur, author, & motivational speaker.

Speech is a shadow of action. (Deeds are fruits, words are but leaves.)
- French Proverb

It was my care to make my life illustrious not by words more than by deeds.
- Sophocles 497 BC – 405 BC; Ancient Greek playwright.

I'm okay, you're okay. Now let's go to work.
- Lyanla Vanzant 1953 - ; American inspirational speaker.

~Work & Action~

Nothing will work unless you do.

- Maya Angelou (Marguerite Ann Johnson) 1928 - ; American author & poet.

The secret of getting ahead is getting started.

- Mark Twain (Samuel Langhorne Clemens) 1835-1910; American author & humorist.

Nothing will ever be attempted if all possible objections must be overcome first.

-Samuel Johnson 1709 – 1784; English writer, poet, essayist, critic, editor, & author of the first English dictionary.

One's action ought to come out of an achieved stillness: not to be a mere rushing on.

- D.H. Lawrence 1885 – 1930; English novelist, poet, playwright, essayist, painter, & critic.

Whatever your life's work is, do it well. A man should do his job so well that the living, the dead, and the unborn could do it no better.

- Dr. Martin Luther King, Jr. (Michael King) 1929 - 1968; American clergyman, minister, civil rights activist. Nobel Peace Prize, Presidential Medal of Freedom, & Congressional Gold Medal recipient.

Quality is not an act, it is a habit.

- Aristotle 384 BC – 322 BC; Greek philosopher, polymath, & one of the fathers of Western philosophy.

He who does not work is without food.

(He that will not work shall not eat. Without due effort one is not entitled to the fruits of the work.)
- Roman Proverb

Vision without execution is hallucination.

- Thomas A. Edison 1847 – 1931; American inventor & businessman.

~Work & Action~

I want to be thoroughly used up when I die, for the harder I work the more I live. I rejoice in life for its own sake.
- *George Bernard Shaw 1856 – 1950; Irish playwright, cofounder of London School of Economics, critic, journalist, Nobel Prize winner, & Oscar winner.*

The wise man bridges the gap by laying out the path by means of which he can get from where he is to where he wants to go.
- *J.P. (John Pierpont) Morgan 1837 – 1913; American financier, banker, & philanthropist.*

Leisure is the time for doing something useful. This leisure the diligent person will obtain the lazy one never.
- *Benjamin Franklin 1706 – 1790; American politician, One of the founding fathers of the U.S., polymath, author, postmaster, scientist, musician, inventor, statesmen, critic, & diplomat.*

Hunger is not your aunt (it will not bring you a pie). (If you are in need, help yourself and don't count on situation improving by itself. One cannot (or should not) expect to benefit without making some effort.)
- *Russian Proverb*

Good actions give strength to ourselves and inspire good actions in others.
- *Plato 428 BC – 347 BC; Greek philosopher, mathematician, founder of Academy of Athens (the first institute of higher learning), student of Socrates & teacher of Aristotle.*

Everyone who's ever taken a shower has an idea. It's the person who gets out of the shower, dries off and does something about it who makes a difference.
- *Nolan Bushnell 1943 - ; American engineer, entrepreneur, inventor of the video game "Pong", founder of Atari, Inc., & founder of Chuck E. Cheese.*

~Work & Action~

There is joy in work. There is no happiness except in the realization that we have accomplished something.

- Henry Ford 1863 – 1947; American industrialist, founder of the Ford Motor Company, & developer of the assembly line.

Henry Ford 1863 – 1947: American industrialist, founder of the Ford Motor Company, & developer of the assembly line. *Ford revolutionized transportation and American industry by developing methods of mass production and high wages for workers known as "Fordism". While as an engineer at Edison Illuminating Company, Ford experimented with gasoline engines. With the help of wealthy investors Ford started the Henry Ford Company in 1901. Due to various disagreements, Ford left the company a year later. The remaining investors renamed the company the Cadillac Automobile Company. Ford then partnered with Alexander Y. Malcomson to form Ford & Malcomson, Ltd. They contracted with John and Horace Dodge to supply parts for the new company. Later in 1903 the Dodge's, Malcomson, and Ford would partner to incorporate the Ford Motor Company.*

The only way to do great work is to love what you do. If you haven't found it yet, keep looking. Don't settle.

- Steve Jobs 1955 – 2011; American inventor, entrepreneur, marketer, & co-founder of Apple Inc.

289

~Work & Action~

Better is the enemy of good. (The aim for perfection or mastery might slow down progress.)
- *Italian Proverb*

People who work sitting down get paid more than people who work standing up.
- *Frederic Ogden Nash 1902 – 1971; American poet.*

You can't use up creativity. The more you use, the more you have.
- *Maya Angelou (Marguerite Ann Johnson) 1928 - ; American author & poet.*

Hard work gives life meaning. Everyone needs to work hard at something to feel good about themselves. Every job can be done well and every day has its satisfactions.
- *Oseola McCarty 1908 – 1999; American washerwomen that forewent luxuries of life so she could save & upon her death established a scholarship trust for deserving students with her life savings.*

Fires can't be made with dead embers, nor can enthusiasm be stirred by spiritless men. Enthusiasm in our daily work lightens effort and turns even labor into pleasant tasks.
- *James A. Baldwin 1924 – 1987; American playwright, novelist, essayist, poet, critic, & civil rights activist.*

Jack of all trades and a master of none.
- *German Proverb*

Opportunities are usually disguised as hard work, so most people don't recognize them.
- *Ann Landers (Esther Pauline Lederer) 1918 – 2002; American advice columnist.*

An unfulfilled vocation drains the color from a man's entire existence.
- *Honore de Balzac 1799 – 1850; French playwright & novelist.*

~Work & Action~

Little by little the bird makes his nest.
(Many incremental changes will eventually make a significant difference.)
- *Haitian Proverb*

The price one pays for pursuing any profession, or calling, is an intimate knowledge of its ugly side.
- *James A. Baldwin 1924 – 1987; American playwright, novelist, essayist, poet, critic, & civil rights activist.*

Pray as though everything depended on God. Work as though everything depended on you.
- *Saint Augustine (Augustine of Hippo) 354 – 430; Ancient Roman theologian, author, philosopher, & developed the idea of the central Catholic Church & original sin.*

If you want to be the best, you've got to work harder than anybody else.
-*Sammy Davis Jr. 1925 – 1990; American singer, dancer, & civil rights activist.*

A man is not idle because he is absorbed in thought. There is a visible labor and there is an invisible labor.
- *Victor Hugo 1802 – 1885; French poet, novelist, & playwright.*

It seems the harder I work, the more luck I have.
- *Thomas Jefferson 1743 – 1826; One of the founding fathers of U.S., the principal author of the Declaration of Independence, & 3rd president of U.S.*

I don't wait for moods. You accomplish nothing if you do that. Your mind must know it has got to get down to work.
- *Pearl S. Buck 1892 – 1973; American writer, novelist, Pulitzer Prize recipient, & Nobel Prize in Literature recipient.*

The journey of a thousand miles must begin with a small step.
- *Chinese Proverb*

~Work & Action~

Nothing is really work unless you would rather be doing something else.
- James M. Barrie 1860 – 1937; Scottish author, dramatist, & creator of "Peter Pan".

The average person puts only 25% of his energy and ability into his work. The world takes off its hat to those who put in more than 50% of their capacity, and stands on its head for those few and far between souls who devote 100%.
- Andrew Carnegie 1835 – 1919; Scottish American industrialist & philanthropists.

All wealth is the product of labor.
- John Locke 1632 – 1704; English philosopher & physician.

He that rises late must trot all day.
- Benjamin Franklin 1706 – 1790; American politician, One of the founding fathers of the U.S., polymath, author, postmaster, scientist, musician, inventor, statesmen, critic, & diplomat.

The first man gets the oyster; the second man gets the shell.
- Andrew Carnegie 1835 – 1919; Scottish American industrialist & philanthropists.

The test of character is the amount of strain it can bear.
- Charles Hamilton Houston 1895 – 1950; American lawyer, civil rights activist, & played a significant role in dismantling Jim Crow laws.
- Unknown

Great thoughts speak only to the thoughtful mind, but great actions speak to all Mankind.
- Emily P. Bissell 1861 – 1948; American social worker & activist.

~Work & Action~

Do what you can, where you are, with what you have.

- Theodore (Teddy) Roosevelt, Jr. 1858 – 1919; American politician, 26th President of the U.S. & Nobel Peace Prize winner.

Theodore (Teddy) Roosevelt, Jr.1858 – 1919; American politician, 26th President of the U.S. & Nobel Peace Prize winner. *Known for his personality, extensive range of interests, many achievements, and poignant leadership, Roosevelt was a naturalist, explorer, hunter, author, soldier, and politician. He is a true example of a man that took life by the horns and experienced everything to the fullest. As a sickly child, Roosevelt adopted a strenuous life to overcome his weakness. As President, he put the nation's power behind the completion of the Panama Canal, sent a naval fleet around the world to demonstrate America's new military might, and negotiated an end to the Russo-Japanese War, which he won the Nobel Peace Prize for. Ranked as one of the greatest U.S. Presidents, he is immortalized on Mt. Rushmore alongside George Washington, Thomas Jefferson, and Abraham Lincoln.*

Let me say to you workers, whenever you are engaged in work that serves humanity and is for the building up of humanity, it has dignity, it has worth.

- Dr. Martin Luther King, Jr. (Michael King) 1929 - 1968; American clergyman, minister, civil rights activist. Nobel Peace Prize, Presidential Medal of Freedom, & Congressional Gold Medal recipient.

Do not leave for others what you can do yourself. (For what thou canst do thyself, rely not on another.)
- *German Proverb*

Whatever good things we build end up building us.
- *Jim Rohn 1930 – 2009; American entrepreneur, author, & motivational speaker.*

The end of labor is to gain leisure.
- *Aristotle 384 BC – 322 BC; Greek philosopher, polymath, & one of the fathers of Western philosophy.*

Who does not want to dig the land shall have nothing but weed.
- *German Proverb*

The eye of the master will do more work than both his hands.
- *Benjamin Franklin 1706 – 1790; American politician, One of the founding fathers of the U.S., polymath, author, postmaster, scientist, musician, inventor, statesmen, critic, & diplomat.*

What works best is delegating authority, learning you cannot do everything, and some people can do it better.
- *Willi Smith 1948 – 1987; American fashion designer.*

Procrastination is the thief of time.
- *English Proverb*

Thunder is good, thunder is impressive; but it is lightning that does the work.
- *Mark Twain (Samuel Langhorne Clemens) 1835-1910; American author & humorist.*

It is the set of the sails, not the direction of the wind that determines which way we will go.
- *Jim Rohn 1930 – 2009; American entrepreneur, author, & motivational speaker.*

Index:

This index has been intentionally left blank. Wisdom comes from many sources. It is not wise to only follow one author.

Enlightenment requires that we keep an open mind.

Thank You for reading this book. If you have a good quote that you feel is left out or want to contact me:

misekabooks@gmail.com
Facebook: M.I. Seka
Twitter: @misekabooks
Linkedin: M.I. Seka

Printed in Great Britain
by Amazon